D1201789

BUILDING
EQUITABLE
CITIES

HOW TO DRIVE ECONOMIC MOBILITY AND REGIONAL GROWTH

Janis Bowdler | Henry Cisneros | Jeffrey Lubell
Foreword by Patrick L. Phillips

JPMORGAN CHASE & CO.

Recommended bibliographic listing:

Bowdler, Janis, Henry Cisneros, and Jeffrey Lubell. *Building Equitable Cities: How to Drive Economic Mobility and Regional Growth*. Washington, DC: Urban Land Institute, 2017.

ISBN: 9-780-87420-410-0

Urban Land Institute
2001 L St., NW, Suite 200
Washington, DC 20036

About the Urban Land Institute

THE URBAN LAND INSTITUTE is a global, member-driven organization comprising more than 40,000 real estate and urban development professionals dedicated to advancing the Institute's mission of providing leadership in the responsible use of land and creating and sustaining thriving communities worldwide.

ULI's interdisciplinary membership represents all aspects of the industry, including developers, property owners, investors, architects, urban planners, public officials, real estate brokers, appraisers, attorneys, engineers, financiers, and academics. Established in 1936, the Institute has a presence in the Americas, Europe, and Asia Pacific regions, with members in 76 countries.

The extraordinary impact that ULI makes on land use decision making is based on its members sharing expertise on a variety of factors affecting the built environment, including urbanization, demographic and population changes, new economic drivers, technology advancements, and environmental concerns.

Peer-to-peer learning is achieved through the knowledge shared by members at thousands of convenings each year that reinforce ULI's position as a global authority on land use and real estate. In 2016 alone, more than 1,700 events were held in 250 cities around the world.

Drawing on the work of its members, the Institute recognizes and shares best practices in urban design and development for the benefit of communities around the globe.

More information is available at uli.org. Follow ULI on Twitter, Facebook, LinkedIn, and Instagram.

ULI SENIOR EXECUTIVES

Patrick L. Phillips
Global Chief Executive Officer

Michael Terseck
Chief Financial Officer/Chief Administrative Officer

Cheryl Cummins
Global Governance Officer

Ralph Boyd
Chief Executive Officer ULI Americas

Lisette van Doorn
Chief Executive Officer ULI Europe

John Fitzgerald
Chief Executive Officer ULI Asia Pacific

Kathleen B. Carey
President and Chief Executive Officer ULI Foundation

Adam Smolyar
Chief Marketing and Membership Officer

Stockton Williams
Executive Vice President Content

Steve Ridd
Executive Vice President Global Business Operations

ULI PROJECT STAFF

Stockton Williams
Executive Vice President Content

Rosemarie Hepner
Director ULI Terwilliger Center for Housing

James A. Mulligan
Senior Editor/Manuscript Editor

Betsy Van Buskirk
Creative Director

John Hall Design Group
Book Designer

Craig Chapman
Senior Director, Publishing Operations

About the Authors

JANIS BOWDLER is the global head of community development, small business, and financial health strategies within Global Philanthropy for JPMorgan Chase & Co., a leader in corporate philanthropy that dedicates about $250 million a year to driving inclusive growth. Bowdler joined JPMorgan Chase in 2013, and under her leadership, the firm has developed innovative private sector solutions to connect distressed communities, underserved individuals, and entrepreneurs from around the world with the resources, expertise, and opportunities necessary to grow and prosper. A proud Latina, wife, and mother, Bowdler has written and spoken extensively about economic mobility for Latino families and other communities of color.

HENRY CISNEROS is chairman and cofounder of CityView, which invests in urban residential real estate projects, and is chairman of the executive committee of Siebert Cisneros Shank, a national public and corporate markets finance firm. Cisneros served four terms as mayor of San Antonio and was secretary of the U.S. Department of Housing and Urban Development under President Bill Clinton. He is vice chair of Habitat for Humanity International and a member of the board of the Bipartisan Policy Center and the Urban Institute in Washington.

JEFFREY LUBELL is the director of housing and community initiatives at Abt Associates, a mission-driven, global leader in research, evaluation, and program implementation in the fields of health, social, and environmental policy. From 2006 through August 2013, Lubell was the executive director of the Center for Housing Policy, a nonprofit research organization affiliated with the National Housing Conference. He also has been director of the Policy Development Division in the U.S. Department of

Housing and Urban Development's Office of Policy Development and Research, a housing policy associate at the Center on Budget and Policy Priorities, and an independent consultant.

PATRICK L. PHILLIPS is the global chief executive officer of the Urban Land Institute. Since taking the chief executive position in 2009, Phillips has overseen an expansion of ULI's global reach, guiding the Institute's focus on creating thriving communities in rapidly urbanizing countries. Under his leadership, ULI's program of work has grown steadily to encompass a variety of economic, demographic, societal, and environmental issues that are reshaping urban development worldwide in the 21st century. Phillips is a frequent speaker on urban development issues and is the author or coauthor of eight books and numerous articles.

Contents

Foreword

THE REVITALIZATION OF THE NATION'S CENTRAL CITIES is one of the great success stories of late-20th-century America. Cities have reinvented themselves as magnets for human capital and centers of innovation. As public safety and the delivery of public services have steadily improved, a new generation of city dwellers has taken up residence in downtowns and close-in neighborhoods, and a previously suburban generation has rediscovered the appeal of city living. This migration has been supported by a wave of new public investment in transit and cultural and recreational amenities.

Jobs have followed, reversing, briefly, the longtime trend of suburbs outpacing city centers in employment growth. More recently, as the economic recovery has gathered steam, peripheral areas are again growing faster, but the gap is far narrower than in previous decades. Further, strong economic drivers, including universities and medical institutions, continue to provide a durable competitive advantage to cities.

A series of recent high-profile corporate relocations have reinforced the notion that competing in the 21st century means providing what a highly mobile, knowledge-based workforce wants: a lively, dense, amenity-rich urban environment. This demand is reflected both in the pace of new urban development and in rising downtown housing values, which have outpaced suburban price increases in recent years, a trend even more pronounced in the nation's largest and strongest metro areas. Walkable, mixed-use urban neighborhoods have shown a demonstrable market premium, an advantage even larger than that enjoyed by the suburbs during the great wave of metropolitan expansion in the 1970s and 1980s.

This is all well known to members of the Urban Land Institute. ULI has been tracking these trends for years and has long advocated for, as stated in the organization's mission, "the responsible use of land to create and sustain thriving communities." For most of the organization's existence, this has translated into a positive view of density, to thinking about transportation and land use together, to finding creative approaches to mixed-use development, and to finding common ground between the public and private sectors to produce balanced metropolitan growth. At the root of all this is a deeply held belief that how we build cities matters. ULI members aim to improve the ability of the built environment to foster human well-being.

Yet despite much progress in advancing these ideas over the past 80 years, the benefits of the recent urban revival have bypassed many. Economist Jed Kolko's recent work has shown that only the richest fifth of the population, for example, has become more urbanized. The bottom 60 percent of the country's income groups—and especially the lowest-income households that make up the bottom tenth—are far less likely to live in a walkable urban neighborhood than other groups. Education makes a difference, too, Kolko has found: people with college degrees are moving in, and working-class families are moving out. Unsurprisingly, most of the newly urban households are childless.

Walkable urbanism is aimed mainly at upper-income households and is most fully expressed in America's most educated, affluent metro areas, as Chris Leinberger's research and the successful projects of countless ULI members have demonstrated. In part because of this, walkable urban places mainly benefit the "winners" in the knowledge economy and, as Richard Florida has observed, reflect deep socioeconomic divides in metro areas.

This sorting-out process is not necessarily voluntary. Gentrification is occurring in more places, on a larger scale, and at a faster pace than ever before. This phenomenon—displacement of longtime residents and businesses due to new investment and rising occupancy costs—is not new, and has both beneficial and negative consequences. This most recent wave is more closely linked with rising rents and home values than previous waves. Data from the U.S. Department of Housing and Urban Development, for example, show a significantly higher proportion of lower-cost city neighborhoods experiencing rapid spikes in rents over the past ten years than in the previous decade. ULI members in our district councils have consistently put housing affordability—and the attendant legal and political challenges of securing entitlements for new projects—at the top of the list of development challenges in their cities.

The result is that concentrated poverty has worsened. By 2014, twice as many households lived in neighborhoods with poverty rates of at least 40 percent as did in 2000, according to the Brookings Institution. Despite increased attention to suburban and rural poverty, poor households remain most prevalent in urban centers. Fully three-quarters of poor people live in big cities, even though suburban poverty is growing much faster. And lower-income African American households are more than twice as likely as white households to live in neighborhoods with concentrated poverty.

ULI has traditionally focused its mission through the lens of market-based capitalism guided by intelligent public policy. And in this case, there is a strong business case for the subject of this book—equitable growth and inclusive prosperity.

Children and families, workers at all skill levels, companies and local economies, and entire regions can benefit from development policies, patterns, and practices that foster economic opportunity and mobility. The evidence shows, for example, that when kids move to lower-poverty areas, they are more likely to attend college and have higher incomes as adults. They are also less likely to become single parents.

Workers and their employers are better off when communities offer both high-skill and low-skill jobs. Places with large differences between urban and suburban wages and skill levels tend to show lower economic productivity and lower overall income growth. Easier access to jobs in booming industries leads to stronger wage gains at all skill levels.

And, according to research by the Federal Reserve Bank of Cleveland, regions that are more equitable and inclusive by various measures are better able to maintain healthy rates of growth. Metro regions with higher levels of inequality are less likely to sustain healthy economic growth over time. Political fragmentation and residential segregation by race and income further weaken regional economic resilience.

The Urban Land Institute undertook this project because we are convinced that real estate developers and investors and local governments—the core of ULI's membership—must lead. It is clear, for now at least, that the federal government believes that state and local governments are better positioned to serve their communities than federal agencies. But the states are also less likely to help. ULI members frequently note a persistent urban/rural divide in state legislatures that results in policies inimical to healthy urban communities and local autonomy. Ultimately, of course, people in cities and their elected leaders want control over their own destinies, and local regulatory policies can have a profound effect on housing affordability, economic mobility, and income inequality.

Increasingly, progressive activists and the business community are not aligned on the impact of zoning and land use regulation on housing supply and affordability. The attendant friction hampers the ability of people to move to areas offering better-paying jobs or higher-performing schools. Reducing geographic mobility limits economic productivity and entrenches inequality. Recent ULI work has focused on regulatory reform as one means of addressing the spiraling cost of producing affordable housing.

In some cases, this concern has translated into counterproductive proposals. The recently defeated Measure S ballot initiative in Los Angeles, for example, would have effectively instituted a moratorium on major real estate development projects in the city. Other barriers to development are becoming common, either through regulation or through community resistance. But such approaches cannot be the answer. The development community is not the enemy, and restricting development does little to address the underlying problems.

Instead, the examples outlined in this book aim to arrive at better, more equitable, and more economically productive outcomes. We know what we should strive for: lower levels of segregation by race and income, a reduction in income inequality, more kids living in two-parent households, less crime, and better schools. This is the common ground upon which policy makers and the business community can come together to find solutions. ULI members are eager to find and advance innovative, practical solutions that harness the power of entrepreneurs, in a framework of strategic public investment, to help break the cycles of disadvantage that perpetuate inequality in our communities.

Patrick L. Phillips

Preface

NOT LONG AGO, many business leaders likely would have skipped over a book about how cities can promote economic mobility. They may well have considered it an interesting and important topic, but one that was in the purview of policy makers, urban planners, and community advocates, not of corporate executives. I am proud of how rapidly this is changing.

Across the private sector, there is growing recognition that the disparity between the haves and have-nots that has characterized our cities for so long is not just a challenge to our social fabric, but also a threat to our nation's economic progress. When individuals are unable to find jobs that offer a path to financial security, when entrepreneurs cannot launch or expand their companies, and when our neighbors are cut off from opportunity, unable to fulfill their potential and left frustrated and disillusioned, communities suffer. Economies suffer. And by extension, business suffers.

Even cities with hot economies today run the risk of becoming less resilient and sluggish if their top-line growth and prosperity allow groups of residents to be left behind or pushed out. As a result, it has become clear to companies like JPMorgan Chase & Co. that helping create greater economic opportunity is not simply the right thing to do; it is in our self-interest. No business can outgrow the economy of its communities.

The private sector not only has a vested interest, but also can make a real contribution to fostering opportunity—in ways far beyond and with greater impact than the traditional model of simply bringing dollars to the table. There is no one-size-fits-all approach, but companies can and should draw on their full range of resources—from the skills and ingenuity of their people to the technological and operational capacity of their enterprises—and apply them in ways that support and accelerate cities' efforts to catalyze economic mobility for their residents.

For some businesses, this might mean aligning their relocation or expansion strategies to advance cities' broader revitalization efforts. Other companies are rethinking their products, services, and delivery models to better meet the needs of underserved consumers. Still others are investing in education and training programs that help local workers land high-quality jobs—while also feeding the talent pipeline that keeps their business and the local economy competitive.

For our part at JPMorgan Chase, we are actively leveraging our core business, deep insight into the economy, and the expertise of our people—coupled with our investment and philanthropic capital—to drive inclusive growth in cities around the world. This includes jump-starting locally driven solutions for revitalizing distressed neighborhoods, connecting underserved entrepreneurs with much-needed capital and resources, arming disadvantaged young people with the skills to compete for today's good jobs, and helping families secure their financial future.

The pressing need to expand opportunities for individuals to move up the economic ladder may not be a new problem, but it requires new solutions. The pages that follow outline a number of successful strategies cities around the country have implemented to break down the barriers to economic mobility, but they should not be read as a prescription for a solo endeavor for mayors and city councils. On the contrary, I am convinced that collaboration across the public, private, and nonprofit sectors is *the* critical success factor. Government and nonprofit organizations cannot solve these challenges alone. The business community can and must be part of the solution.

This book, then, is also a call for business and civic leaders to join forces at the local level to advance tailored strategies that will lead to meaningful change. We have seen firsthand how this collaborative approach is working in cities around the globe, and we hope to partner with others in the private sector who share this vision. If we all work together—each sector marshaling its unique resources and doing what it does best—we can make true and lasting progress toward closing the opportunity gap in our cities.

Janis Bowdler

Preface

Equity: A Natural Next Step in the Evolution of Cities

OVER THE PAST 40 YEARS, I have had the privilege of observing the evolution of U.S. cities from a range of perspectives. I have seen cities become more capable and sophisticated in nurturing both a healthy regional economy and the economic and social capacity of their residents. While there is more they can do to accelerate the trend, cities increasingly are working to foster the conditions that lead to economic mobility, a vital component of broader efforts to create a more equitable society. The concerted effort to promote economic mobility that we recommend in this volume is consistent with this trend—a logical next step in the evolution of cities.

Of course, U.S. cities have been evolving throughout the history of our country. In this preface, I provide a brief overview of cities' progression and show how promoting economic mobility and other components of the equity agenda are a natural and important role for cities in the 21st century.

The Historical Progression of U.S. Cities toward Equity Goals

Cities and their municipal governments have been an integral part of American progress since the founding of our nation. Early in American history, cities such as Boston and New York City assumed important roles as centers of commerce, ports of trade, and staging areas for the immigrant populations that swelled the nation's population. From the early to mid-1800s, city governments incorporated and organized themselves to provide basic municipal services such as police and fire security, street maintenance, sanitation, and water distribution.

As the number and scale of cities grew and new mechanical devices could be applied to the urban quality of life, city governments offered or supervised the establishment of electric utilities to generate and distribute power for street lighting and for the use of households and businesses. By the latter years of the 19th century, city governments were using the latest engineering techniques to design flood control projects, construct ports and levees, plan parks and public auditoriums, establish libraries, and build educational institutions, including public schools and colleges.

In the early years of the 20th century, city governments directly addressed a new range of issues related to their increasing populations. Many were spurred by reformers such as Jacob Riis, who described the squalor of urban living conditions, to build better housing to replace the poorly built and unhealthy tenements that crowded many city neighborhoods. And with the advent of the New Deal and its strategy of stimulating the economy through public investment in massive public improvements, city governments joined the federal government to provide public housing and build large-scale public works such as dams and urban water reservoirs, green spaces and recreation areas, and thruways to facilitate the movement of motorized traffic.

While the most urgent intent of the Franklin Roosevelt administration was to increase employment, the crisis of the Great Depression uncovered the dire conditions of poverty, hunger, illness, and aged frailty that affected millions of Americans. During the Depression, cities became full partners with the federal government in the nation's first equity agenda and became the tip of the spear for programs to generate employment, ensure new social safety nets, and create a legacy of lasting public improvements. The immensity of the economic crisis and the shock to the nation's conscience embedded concepts of equality, fairness, and opportunity in the fabric of the nation's social, political, and economic institutions for generations thereafter.

In the years following World War II, city governments participated in the growth of the American economy through innovations in local economic development. City governments invested in massive convention centers, collaborated to provide sports stadiums for the expanding public interest in professional football and baseball, and assumed catalytic roles in the strengthening of urban downtowns. City leaders led the way in clearing spaces for corporate office headquarters, extending mass transit via rail and subway systems, and explicitly spurring urban development using tax abatements and urban renewal.

As the nation's economy began to deindustrialize in the 1960s and manufacturing plants left urban core areas, city populations increasingly moved to the suburbs. Policy makers, scholars, and the media declared an "urban crisis." Social commentators, such as Michael Harrington in his 1962 book *The Other America: Poverty in the United States*, painted a stark picture of inequality and human suffering. The civil rights movement drew attention to the racial dimensions of the urban transformation as poverty became more concentrated, neighborhoods were segregated by race, and jobs and wages in the cities declined.

President Lyndon Johnson's Great Society initiatives committed to a wide range of human services programs that, though they were initiated and funded at the federal level, required city governments and nonprofit organizations in the cities to deliver the programs at the local level. The Johnson administration updated the Roosevelt equity agenda and declared a War on Poverty in urban and rural communities. The scope of its human services programs was broad, including early child development, job training, K–12 education assistance, health clinics, and programs for seniors. Neighborhood antipoverty efforts and organizations such as the Model Cities Program and the community development corporations sponsored by the Office of Economic Opportunity built on and expanded human services traditionally offered by churches and settlement houses. Those human-capital investments and the accompanying mobilization of community participation harnessed the momentum of civil rights–era laws, such as the Voting Rights Act, and of numerous Great Society initiatives in education, health services, and income security.

Channels of Funding for Equity Programs

In the 50 years since the rollout of the Great Society programs, significant change has taken place in the funding channels for programs with equity objectives.

Some programs have relied on local governmental budgets principally from city and county governments, school districts, and community colleges. State governments have been participants in equity programs, particularly through their departments of health and education. The federal government has remained a major source of funding for human services programs through the specific channels, or silos, of the cabinet departments. Examples include Community Development Block Grants and the HOME Program from the Department of Housing and Urban Development, Economic Development Administration initiatives from the Department of Commerce, health clinic initiatives from the Department of Health and Human Services, school lunch programs from the Department of Education, funding for manpower training from the Department of Labor, and rural development programs from the Department of Agriculture.

In addition to government agencies, philanthropic foundations have played major roles over the years in supporting new approaches to delivery of human services. The Ford Foundation, the Rockefeller Foundation, and the Annie E. Casey Foundation, for example, along with area foundations in many metropolitan regions, have contributed a steady stream of resources to human services over many decades. Corporate partnerships and contributions in areas such as child care, youth programs, and educational interventions have expanded the funds available for needed human services in communities. Detroit's steady comeback has required a combination of engaged leadership and financial resources from the Kresge Foundation, JPMorgan Chase, and Quicken Loans. Many cities have raised funds broadly through United Way campaigns and benefited from local civic involvement by volunteers working at the grassroots level. The combination of these massive commitments represents financial resources and human energies available for local equity programs coming through many channels of distribution and focusing on specific neighborhoods, organizations, and needs.

Local Delivery Capacities for Equity Programs

On the receiving end of these resource channels is an equally wide array of delivery and execution entities. The range of government and nonprofit organizations committed to enhancing opportunity and equality is wide.

It includes church initiatives such as Catholic Charities, various Protestant ministries, Jewish community centers, and other church commitments to child care, homeless services, and senior services. Nonprofit organizations of many kinds are in the field. Some are community-based organizations with strong advocacy commitments, such as the Industrial Areas Foundation. In most metropolitan areas, there are strong and experienced community development corporations and more recently community development financial institutions; both types of organization have received funding from the federal level to work in designated subareas of cities or in rural communities but augment those funds with local resources.

Most municipal governments have extensive human services departments that operate senior nutrition programs and various forms of training initiatives. In the education arena, school districts offer not just traditional K–12 programs, but also after-school programs, literacy initiatives, compensatory education, and increasingly early pre-K instruction. They are joined in the education space by community colleges, four-year colleges, and universities in access-to-college programs, including scholarships. In most communities, small, neighborhood-level, even block-level volunteer programs work with youths, assist senior citizens, feed the homeless, repair deteriorated homes, and provide street patrols, surviving on minimal budgets funded locally.

Cities as Leaders in Efforts to Promote Economic Mobility

There are many reasons why cities can be effective leaders of efforts to promote economic mobility and other equity initiatives. Cities can frame appropriate responses because they are close to the problem. City leaders are in the best position to understand the makeup of poverty in their respective communities. City governments can be coordinators, in the sense of orchestra conductors, of the disparate capabilities and resources that exist at the local level to combat poverty. They need not be the initiator in every case or the sole provider of resources, but they can frame the local context, create a network of action to engage existing organizations and streams of funding, and weave them into a coherent response. The task is to match the delivery capabilities, traditions, specializations, and resources of organizations with the spectrum of needs identified within the community. Cities are institutions of permanence and therefore have the capability to set up long-term arrangements. They also can respond to the scale of the effort in that they have responsibility for every neighborhood and every district of the city and can make sure that the entire geography of the city is covered.

Though cities are well positioned to help residents move up the economic ladder, and many are actively engaged in doing so, there is more that cities could and should be doing. In this volume, we have compiled a range of recommendations for how cities and their partners can use place-based and people-based approaches to promote economic mobility. We hope that these ideas will be helpful both as guidance and inspiration for cities interested in more actively promoting an equity agenda.

In addition to this practical guidance on how to promote economic mobility, we also provide suggestions in our final chapter for how cities can develop a strategic plan for promoting this mobility as part of a broader equity agenda, along with the operational infrastructure needed to advance that plan. While a growing number of cities are focusing explicitly on an equity agenda and some have appointed chief equity officers, no city government in the United States today has created an overarching equity umbrella and assembled under it the myriad governmental and independent efforts involved in equity programs. It is a city leadership task that can be achieved. It would apply the necessary scale and coordination of effort to combat the widespread, persistent, and accelerating growth of inequality as it manifests itself in America today.

Engaging cities as leaders in a national strategy of combatting inequality is America's best hope for ensuring that our historical experience of progressively building a more fair society continues and that our ongoing quest for a more equitable society will drive our future.

Henry Cisneros

Acknowledgments

IN ADDITION TO THE REFERENCES CITED in the text, the authors and the Urban Land Institute thank the following for their contributions to this book: Mona Angel, Sawmill Community Land Trust; Ted Archer, JPMorgan Chase & Co.; Janie Barrera, LiftFund; Sherri Boone, Strive-Partnership; Colleen Briggs, JPMorgan Chase & Co.; Jessica Brooks, New York City Department of Consumer Affairs Office of Financial Empowerment; Mary Alice Cisneros; Rebecca Cohen, Abt Associates; Lucrecia Cross, Siebert Cisneros Shank & Co. LLC; Ricardo Estrada, Instituto del Progreso Latino; Emily Foote-Huth, Cleveland Foundation; Renee Glover, the Catalyst Group LLC.; Megan Hyla, King County Housing Authority; John Roach, City of Detroit; Donna Shafer, Cityline Partners; Whitney Smith, JP Morgan Chase & Co.; Jennie Sparandara, JPMorgan Chase & Co.; Claudia Vasquez, Cisneros Miramontes LLC; Michael Verchot, University of Washington Consulting and Business Development Center; and Duncan Wallace, Wallace & Company. Any errors or omissions are the responsibility of the authors and the Urban Land Institute.

BUILDING
EQUITABLE
CITIES

CHAPTER 1

Introduction

THIS BOOK IS A *CALL TO ACTION*—a call for cities to recognize and realize their potential to catalyze opportunity for their residents by playing a leadership role in efforts to foster economic mobility.

Economic mobility is the ability of an individual to move up the economic ladder. A strong focus on economic mobility is in the self-interest of cities: cities are more likely to succeed if their residents have the ability to realize their full economic potential. It is also an important means to the end of creating a more equitable society.

This book argues that cities should combine *place-based* and *people-based* strategies to create an environment in which all residents have meaningful opportunities to move up the economic ladder. By assuming this role, cities will not only promote fairness and justice, but also expand and sustain their regional economies.

Place-based and people-based strategies are complementary approaches to promoting economic mobility that together establish an ambitious agenda for U.S. cities.

Place-based strategies are designed to address and overcome the spatial inequities that constrain residents' opportunities according to the zip code in which they live. Place-based strategies focus on ensuring that people of all incomes, races, ethnicities, ages, genders, and abilities have equitable access to the place-based services and resources—such as good schools and safe neighborhoods—essential for maximizing their potential for economic mobility. To create systems that support these outcomes, cities should invest in strategies that (a) strengthen struggling neighborhoods and improve the quality of services they provide and (b) expand the availability of affordable housing in areas that already offer high-quality services and a resource-rich environment.

People-based strategies, in contrast, focus on services not tied to a particular neighborhood, but instead delivered to anyone who needs assistance regardless of where they live. The focus here, in particular, is on systems for strengthening the education, workforce, and financial outcomes that play an important role in helping individuals realize their economic potential.

As outlined in the Henry Cisneros preface, many cities have already begun to make the transition from their traditional role as basic service providers and centers of commerce to their new role as catalysts for economic mobility. Others will follow. Though no single city has combined all the place-based and people-based strategies needed to ensure that residents have equitable opportunities, most of the needed activities have been undertaken in some form somewhere in the United States or overseas. The question is not whether cities can take on this new role, but whether they are ready and willing to do so.

This book makes the case for why cities should focus on promoting economic mobility and suggests a roadmap for how they can do so. The book uses the term *city* in a broad sense to refer not only to the mayor and the agencies he or she directly oversees, but also to other public and quasi-public agencies that operate at the city level, such as the public school system and the public housing authority. This book also uses the term *city* to be inclusive of counties because in many urban areas, counties play a leading role in promoting economic mobility. In addition, efforts to promote economic mobility require strong partnerships between the public sector and the nonprofit, business, and philanthropic communities. Therefore, the focus here is not limited to actions that are wholly public in nature. Ultimately, it takes the coordinated efforts of all sectors— with leadership from the mayor and the support of city council—to make progress on improving economic mobility.

Four chapters follow this Introduction. Chapter 2, "Why Cities Should Focus on Economic Mobility," examines three basic questions:

- **HOW CAN CITIES PROMOTE ECONOMIC MOBILITY?** They can promote economic mobility by combining place-based and people-based strategies to develop systems that maximize residents' economic opportunities. Because the economic success of a city depends on the economic success of its region, cities that care about opportunity, equity, and economic mobility also think and work at the regional scale to support these same elements in the broader metropolitan area.

- **WHY SHOULD CITIES FOCUS ON PROMOTING ECONOMIC MOBILITY?** The ability of individuals to realize their economic potential should not be determined by the color of their skin or the location where they were born or the resources available to their families. Fairness alone is thus ample reason to focus on promoting opportunity and economic mobility. But there is growing evidence that more equitable cities are also more prosperous, achieving stronger and longer-lasting economic growth. So a focus on ensuring that all residents have the ability to move up the economic ladder is also in the self-interest of cities.

- **HOW CAN CITIES MEASURE THEIR PROGRESS?** A city's success in adopting policies and programs to promote economic mobility may be a useful measure of early progress. Ultimately, however, progress should be judged by quantifiable changes in outcomes. A city focused on promoting opportunity and economic mobility should expect to see improvements in incomes, educational achievement, and financial health among low-income households and racial and ethnic minorities, as well as increases in the affordability of housing in resource-rich areas. Such cities should also expect reductions in inequality in each of these domains, as well as reductions in racial and ethnic segregation and in disparities in neighborhood services and amenities.

Chapter 3, "Place-Based Strategies," describes how cities can use place-based strategies to expand residents' opportunities for economic mobility. It has three parts:

- **"FOUR KEY CONTEXTS FOR PLACE-BASED STRATEGIES."** Multiple contexts exist for a city's efforts to implement place-based strategies to promote economic mobility. This chapter discusses four of these contexts: (a) the perspective and experiences of city residents, (b) data on conditions in the city and individual neighborhoods, (c) a city's overall housing strategy, and (d) the Assessment of Fair Housing required by the U.S. Department of Housing and Urban Development (HUD).

- **"REDUCING NEIGHBORHOOD DISPARITIES IN ACCESS TO OPPORTUNITY."** This book addresses two main categories of place-based strategies. The first, covered in this part of chapter 3, focuses on strengthening struggling communities and improving the services and resources provided to residents. Practical guidance is provided on how to address neighborhood-level disparities in such key amenities as public education, public safety, and transportation access to jobs.

- **"INCREASING THE AVAILABILITY OF AFFORDABLE HOUSING IN RESOURCE-RICH AREAS."** The second category of place-based strategy focuses on ensuring that residents of all incomes can afford to live in areas that have (or are likely to soon acquire) proficient schools, safe streets, good access to jobs, and other amenities associated with increased opportunity for children and adults. Drawing on case studies from around the United States, this part of chapter 3 provides practical guidance on how to achieve these goals.

Chapter 4, "People-Based Strategies," provides practical guidance on how cities can use people-based strategies to help residents move up the economic ladder. Among other approaches, cities can provide universal pre-kindergarten, strengthen the quality of the kindergarten-through-12th-grade education system, connect residents to career paths that help them accelerate their progress toward higher-paying jobs, improve access to community college and other post-secondary education programs, help residents build assets and financial capability, and expand the availability of credit for small businesses.

Chapter 5, "Developing Strategic Plans," describes one way to jump-start these efforts—developing an economic mobility plan or equity plan that articulates a comprehensive strategy for achieving these goals. To make progress in increasing economic mobility, cities need to take multiple steps across a range of disciplines. Cities thus need a mechanism for tracking and overseeing implementation of the plan, coordinating the efforts of multiple city departments, and holding the city accountable for results. These efforts should be informed by robust citizen input, including through the creative use of technology to ensure that all voices are heard.

CHAPTER 2

Why Cities Should Focus on Economic Mobility

THIS CHAPTER PROVIDES AN OVERVIEW of how cities can promote economic mobility, describes why this is an important objective, and outlines how cities and regions can measure their progress toward this objective.

How Can Cities Promote Economic Mobility?

Cities can promote economic mobility by combining place-based and people-based strategies to develop systems that maximize residents' ability to climb the economic ladder.

Place-based strategies focus on addressing the disparities in opportunity associated with the zip code in which one lives, seeking to ensure that all residents have access to high-quality schools, safe neighborhoods, and other place-based services and resources essential to individual growth and success.

There are two main approaches for achieving this outcome. The first is to invest in strengthening struggling communities and improving the services and resources provided to neighborhood residents. This book focuses in particular on comprehensive community development strategies that seek to address many challenges simultaneously in order to achieve the scale of change necessary to alter a neighborhood's trajectory; community development spurred by anchor institutions, such as a university or hospital; community benefits agreements that leverage large-scale private development to generate benefits for local residents; and education improvements that address disparities by neighborhood, income, race, and ethnicity.

The second is to use affordable housing strategies to help low-income and minority residents gain access to resource-rich neighborhoods—those that already offer high-performing schools, safe streets, and other important place-based services and amenities. The focus here is on preserving and expanding the availability of affordable homes, increasing the availability of lower-cost housing types, and helping low-income households use vouchers to rent housing in these neighborhoods.

People-based strategies, by contrast, focus on meeting the needs of individuals throughout the city for services that improve their economic opportunities, including education, workforce, and financial services. These include, for example, promoting high-quality jobs that provide a living wage, investing in universal pre-kindergarten, offering career pathways programs, and creating networks that support small businesses and entrepreneurship. Without these and other similar efforts, many individuals will fall through the cracks and be unable to advance economically.

A few examples will help make clear the connection between these two components. Including affordable housing in a new development in a resource-rich area—an important place-based strategy—may help ensure that the neighborhood is diverse, but without people-based strategies like universal pre-K and career pathways programs, the potential for equitable outcomes inherent in this diversity will not be realized. Likewise, efforts to support college access and entrepreneurship are important people-based strategies, but they alone cannot compensate for growing up in a neighborhood that lacks effective schools or is unsafe—amenities addressed by place-based strategies.

In addition to place-based and people-based strategies, two companion elements are necessary for cities to advance economic mobility and increase basic equity.

■ **A PROACTIVE, INCLUSIVE, AND TRANSPARENT PROCESS FOR
DEVELOPING AND IMPLEMENTING POLICIES THAT PROMOTE
ECONOMIC MOBILITY AND INCREASE EQUITY.**[1] Economic mobility and equity do not emerge on their own. They must be planned, translated into achievable and workable policies, and then adopted and implemented. For this to occur, cities need a process that works systematically and incrementally to turn the vision of an equitable city into a reality. This process must be inclusive and transparent—both to ensure its success and because inclusion and transparency will ensure that the policies adopted are as responsive as possible to community needs. A successful process will also require strong leadership from the mayor, city council, business leaders, and others. Even the best-run and most well-intentioned city will need to make changes in order to promote equity, and those changes will not happen without strong and effective leadership.

■ **A REGIONAL PERSPECTIVE.** Cities that see their boundaries as walls are likely to fall short of their goals for economic growth, economic mobility, and equity. In today's economy, regions are the engines of growth, and effective collaboration across jurisdictional boundaries is essential for ensuring a healthy regional economy. Regional collaboration is also necessary to make robust progress toward a more equitable city and region. For example, a career pathways program will be most effective if it links individuals throughout the region with job opportunities throughout the region, rather than focusing only on residents and jobs within city boundaries. Likewise, to ensure spatial equity, affordable housing is needed both in growing, high-demand neighborhoods within the city and in suburban jurisdictions with high-performing schools. Minneapolis and St. Paul provide an instructive example of regional collaboration in the distribution of new affordable housing, working both with each other and with the surrounding suburban counties.

Figure 1: Strategies for Creating an Equitable City

Strategies in this book	Other important efforts
Place-based strategies for promoting economic mobility:	Strategies for expanding democracy and inclusion:
• Comprehensive community development	• Fair elections open to all
• Community benefits agreements	• Inclusion of immigrants in civic life
• Affordable housing strategies	• Inclusion of the lesbian, gay, bisexual, transgender, questioning (LGBTQ) community
• Housing mobility strategies	
People-based strategies for promoting economic mobility:	Strategies for ensuring just policing and court systems
• Education initiatives	Strategies for removing barriers to employment and services:
• Workforce initiatives	• Reentry efforts for ex-offenders
• Financial health initiatives	• Efforts to ensure a diverse municipal workforce
• Support for small businesses and entrepreneurship	• Expanded child care
Strategies for ensuring a proactive, inclusive, and transparent process for promoting economic mobility and equity	Strategies for ensuring universal access to healthy foods and green space
	Strategies for advancing tolerance and respect for cultural differences
	Strategies for ensuring environmental justice and equitable outcomes in health, fire, and safety

Note: The expanded menu of policies identified by PolicyLink for its All-In Cities Initiative (Sarah Treuhaft, *All-in Cities: Building an Equitable Economy from the Group Up* [Oakland, CA: PolicyLink, 2016]) provides a helpful inventory of the broad range of possible strategies a city can pursue to promote equity. Some categories from this inventory have been adapted for the right-hand column of this table.

This book views efforts by cities to promote economic mobility as a subset of the broader activities they undertake to promote equity. Many important activities not covered in this book are included in this broader framework. Unbiased policing, for example, helps ensure that everyone is treated fairly by police. Efforts to prevent recidivism and promote the residential and economic integration of people once jailed help ensure that everyone gets a second chance to contribute to the economy. Inclusion of immigrants in civic life, fair elections open to all, broader representation of diverse communities in municipal employment—these are only a few examples of the steps an equitable city takes to promote fairness. Figure 1 outlines the components of an equitable city covered in this book, as well as those that fall outside its scope; it is drawn from a framework developed by the national research and action institute PolicyLink for its All-In Cities Initiative to define the broad scope of strategies for promoting equity.

Why Should Cities Focus on Promoting Economic Mobility?

Activities to promote economic mobility build on and extend the traditional functions of cities. As outlined in the Cisneros preface, cities historically have focused on providing basic services to accommodate the needs of residents and businesses and on attracting and supporting businesses to expand the economy. A focus on ensuring that residents can realize their economic potential is consistent with cities' interest in strengthening the local economy. The innovation lies in defining what a strong local economy is.

A healthy local economy as measured by a growing job base and rising economic output is an essential component of a successful city. But it is not sufficient on its own. In addition to growing, local economies need to work effectively for as many people as possible. Without an economy that provides opportunities for each individual to reach his or her economic potential, cities not only will be less fair and less inclusive, but also will fall short of their own potential. As discussed later, a growing body of research suggests that cities that are more equitable are also more successful in generating and sustaining economic growth.

Efforts to promote economic mobility have three main benefits: fairness, economic growth, and reduction of concentrated poverty.

FAIRNESS

After decades of fighting for greater fairness and inclusion in the United States, some have grown weary of arguments grounded simply in the basic value of fairness. But arguments for fairness remain as valid and powerful as ever and strongly support efforts to promote economic mobility. There is simply no legitimate reason why opportunity should be determined by the color of one's skin or the accidents of where one was born or the resources available to one's family.

This book is not arguing for giving anyone a handout. It is arguing that all people should have an opportunity to grow up, live, and age in a neighborhood that provides the basic systems they require to realize their economic potential. Many people face barriers to economic inclusion and growth over their lifetime. Though many have access to a wide and varied support system that helps them overcome these obstacles, many others do not. Some of these individuals will succeed notwithstanding a lack of support. But when large numbers of children, adults, and families can be seen falling behind despite strong and, indeed, heroic efforts to move forward, society must recognize that the support systems are broken. And while some may succeed despite the odds, children's futures are too important to trust to a roll of the dice.

In evaluating this argument, remember that fairness is not the same as equality. This book does not argue that cities should seek to ensure that everyone is equal in the sense of having the same income or the same wealth. Rather, it argues that cities should seek to ensure that everyone has an equal opportunity to realize his or her economic potential. In an equitable city, a person's motivation and willingness to work hard will still influence his or her ability to advance economically, as they should. What should not matter is the color of one's skin, one's country of origin, or the income and education level of one's parents.

ECONOMIC GROWTH

Cities that support economic mobility are not only fairer, but also are more successful economically. As a number of prominent researchers have demonstrated, U.S. cities and regions with lower levels of inequality exhibit stronger economic growth and are better able to sustain that growth over time.[2] In a recent analysis, for example, Chris Benner and Manuel Pastor document a strong relationship between income inequality and whether a region will experience sustained economic growth (defined as at least 12 consecutive quarters of rising employment).[3] Their research showed that regions with higher levels of income inequality (as measured by higher Gini coefficients) were substantially less likely to experience and maintain sustained growth between 1990 and 2011.

A working paper prepared for the Federal Reserve Bank of Cleveland also found benefits associated with greater income equality in a study of factors affecting economic growth in U.S. cities similar in size to those in northeast Ohio.[4] (See figure 2.) That research showed that cities with greater income equality and greater racial inclusion experienced greater growth in employment and economic output between 1994 and 2004 than did cities lacking these characteristics. Cities with more income equality also experienced higher growth in per-capital income. Among other conclusions, the researchers found substantial economic benefits associated with having a skilled workforce.

The finding that income inequality has a negative impact on economic growth in U.S. cities and regions mirrors the results of research investigating the relationship of these factors at the international level. For example, a 2014 policy brief by the Organisation for Economic Co-operation and Development (OECD) summarized research on the relationship between these factors in OECD countries: "New OECD analysis suggests that income inequality has a negative and statistically significant impact on medium-term growth."[5] According to the OECD brief, "The evidence is strongly in favour of one particular theory for how inequality affects

Figure 2: Equity and Inclusion Are Drivers of Economic Growth

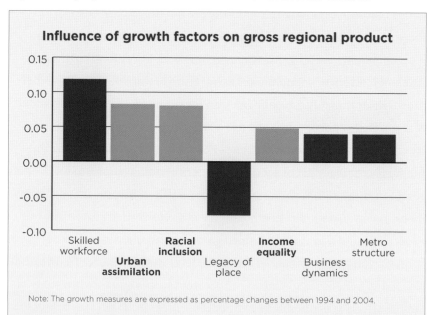

Influence of growth factors on gross regional product

Note: The growth measures are expressed as percentage changes between 1994 and 2004.

A 2006 study by the Reserve Bank of Cleveland of 118 metropolitan areas throughout the United States found that indicators of equitable development and economic mobility exert positive influences on regional employment and economic productivity. *Federal Reserve Bank of Cleveland*

growth: by hindering human capital accumulation, income inequality undermines education opportunities for disadvantaged individuals, lowering social mobility and hampering skills development."[6]

In other words, income inequality may lead to a vicious cycle in which a lack of economic opportunity for low-income individuals leads to slower economic growth because poor workers in a community characterized by inequality do not have the means and cannot see the benefit of investing in their education and skills development. It is also possible that regions characterized by income inequality lack the supports residents need to build human capital and advance economically. Whatever the precise relationship among the three components, it is clear that income equality, economic growth, and supports to promote economic mobility go hand in hand. Cities wanting to maximize their potential for economic growth must invest in the supports needed to allow each individual to achieve his or her own economic potential. These investments will, in turn, reduce income inequality and fuel economic growth.

Chapters 3 and 4 examine strategies cities use to boost economic productivity and growth by strengthening struggling neighborhoods and helping individuals advance economically. One case study focuses on Cleveland, which, after experiencing regional deindustrialization, tapped an array of anchor institutions to revitalize a section of downtown and lay the foundation for inclusive economic growth. Among other strategies, Cleveland combined the medical expertise of the Cleveland Clinic with the engineering capabilities of Case Western Reserve University to develop a nationally significant medical devices cluster. The effort has shown impressive promise in creating sector growth that can support inner-city firms and central-city employment.

As is the case with income inequality, emerging evidence suggests that racial and ethnic segregation may exact an economic toll. A recent study of large U.S. metro areas by the Urban Institute found that African Americans had lower per-capita income and were less educated in regions with higher levels of racial segregation. Applying the findings to the Chicago region, the study estimated that reducing racial segregation in Chicago to levels similar to those experienced in other large metro areas would increase the per capita income of African Americans by 12.4 percent, for an aggregate increase of $4.4 billion.[7] This loss of income exacts a financial toll not only on minority households, but also on cities, which are deprived of the job creation and tax benefits associated with greater and more widely dispersed income growth. Cities likewise suffer when low-income and minority households experience inadequate educational achievement and poor financial health.

Chapter 3 discusses efforts to expand the availability of affordable housing in resource-rich areas, an approach that not only can help individuals gain access to high-quality schools and other neighborhood supports, but also begin to reduce racial and ethnic segregation.

REDUCTION OF CONCENTRATED POVERTY

A final benefit of promoting economic mobility stems from place-based efforts to reduce concentrations of poverty. After declining substantially between 1990 and 2000, the number of people living in areas of concentrated poverty (defined as census tracts with poverty rates of 40 percent or more) has rebounded sharply since 2000 and now far exceeds its previous peak. As of the 2009–2013 American Community Survey, 13.8 million people lived in areas of concentrated poverty, an increase of 91 percent since 2000 and 44 percent since 1990.[8]

As William Julius Wilson observed in his 1987 book *The Truly Disadvantaged*, neighborhoods of concentrated poverty can produce higher rates of violent crime and lower levels of education attainment, marriage, and employment, which reinforce a cycle of poverty that diminishes opportunities for children and perpetuates disadvantage. In high-poverty neighborhoods, Wilson wrote,

> children will seldom interact on a sustained basis with people who are employed or with families that have a steady breadwinner. The net effect is that joblessness, as a way of life, takes on a different social meaning; the relationship between schooling and post-school employment takes on a different meaning. The development of cognitive, linguistic, and other educational and job-related skills necessary for the world of work in the mainstream economy is thereby adversely affected. In such neighborhoods, therefore, teachers become frustrated and do not teach and children do not learn. A vicious cycle is perpetuated through the family, through the community, and through the schools.

By expanding the availability of affordable housing in resource-rich areas and revitalizing struggling neighborhoods, cities can help break this cycle, unlocking the economic potential of residents trapped in a cycle of poverty and allowing the shift of resources from public safety to education and other services that help residents economically.

Quantifying Progress

The people- and place-based strategies discussed in this book should help cities achieve a range of important outcomes, including reduced income inequality, increased educational achievement, and reduced racial/ethnic segregation. To understand whether progress is being made toward these and other key outcomes, cities need to monitor their progress, focusing not only on policy achievements, but also on quantifiable outputs and outcomes.

The following are suggestions on how to measure progress, focusing in particular on measuring quantifiable outcomes. These suggestions should help cities seeking to track their progress while also clarifying the kinds of outcomes they should expect to result from strategies promoting

Environmental Sustainability

Though efforts to boost social mobility and environmental objectives do not always line up perfectly, a city that meets a greater share of the regional demand for housing by increasing the availability of affordable housing can help promote environmental sustainability by reducing energy use and associated greenhouse gas emissions. The benefits stem primarily from the lower energy demands of urban living—compared with suburban living—because of the lower heating/cooling/electricity needs of smaller residences and fewer and shorter car trips.

The inclusion of affordable housing near transit stations can also lead to increased use of transit because lower-income households use transit more than do others. Finally, strategies to improve energy efficiency can both improve the environment by reducing energy use and make housing more affordable by reducing utility expenses.

economic mobility. Though the appendix to this book examines specific ways to measure outcomes, a discussion is included here in order to emphasize the importance of seeking and achieving measurable results.

The results of strategies for promoting economic mobility can be measured in four main ways:

- **PROGRESS IN ADOPTING NEW POLICIES AND PROGRAMS.** As discussed in chapter 5, cities should develop a plan to identify specific policies and programs that they intend to adopt to promote economic mobility. These plans can focus either on economic mobility efforts specifically or on a broader set of efforts to make the city more equitable. Cities should measure their progress in adopting the policies and programs outlined in their plans. Particularly in the early years of implementation, before the effects of the new policies and programs can be expected to show up in outcome data, these procedural achievements may be the best way to measure progress.

- **THE OUTPUTS OF CITY POLICIES.** Once new policies and programs are adopted, the initial measure of their success will be the outputs they produce. Examples include the number of children enrolled in pre-K, the amount of affordable housing built in resource-rich areas, and the number of small businesses assisted in getting access to capital. These are the numbers most commonly reported by cities and others in documenting the results of policies and programs.

- **CHANGES IN KEY OUTCOMES.** Ultimately, progress should be evaluated by gauging whether and to what extent the community is seeing improved outcomes. Key outcomes to measure include household income, educational achievement, household financial health, amount of affordable housing, and reduction of racial/ethnic segregation. The balance of this section and the appendix provide recommendations for how to approach these measurements.

■ **CHANGES IN DISPARITIES BETWEEN NEIGHBORHOODS.** A final area to track is the extent to which disparities between neighborhoods decline over time. Among other neighborhood measures to consider in this domain are school quality, crime, and transportation access to jobs.

Figure 3 summarizes measures communities can use to track progress, citing one or more illustrative metrics for monitoring progress by populations in need and a reduction in inequality.

It may be years before the effects of a new policy can be detected in outcomes for the city as a whole. Ultimately, however, if a city is becoming more equitable, meaningful gains in outcomes should be experienced by households that have struggled economically, such as those in the bottom half of the income distribution, and by racial and ethnic minorities. These gains can occur and be important even if inequality remains high or even increases. At the same time, a city that is becoming more equitable should ultimately expect to see reductions in inequality among its residents—or at least a slowdown in the growth of inequality. A city can experience reductions in inequality even when populations in need are not making absolute progress—for example, because of declines among people at the top of the distribution. By measuring both progress by households in need and reduced inequality—as illustrated by the two columns of outcomes in figure 3—cities can gain a fuller understanding of their progress in becoming more equitable and whether the progress is due to gains among people in the bottom of the distribution or declines at the top, or both.

Where possible, cities should also compare their results with those for the region as a whole. Regional results can provide important context for interpreting city results. Regional outcomes are also of interest in their own right because the ideal result of efforts to create equitable cities would be more equitable outcomes for the broader region, too.

Figure 3: Illustrative Measures for Tracking Progress

Domain	Progress by populations in need	Reduced inequality
Household income	Higher average incomes in bottom half of income distribution	Lower Gini coefficient
Educational achievement	Higher share of low-income households and racial/ethnic minorities meeting minimum standards for math and reading	Smaller gaps in average test scores among households of different races, ethnicities, and incomes
Household financial health	Higher average credit scores for households in the bottom half of the income distribution	Smaller disparities in credit scores among households of different races, ethnicities, and incomes
Amount of affordable housing	Higher share of units in resource-rich areas that are affordable to very low-income households[a]	Smaller gaps in access to resource-rich areas among households of different races, ethnicities, and incomes
Racial/ethnic segregation	Higher percentage of the city's racial and ethnic minority households living in integrated neighborhoods	Lower dissimilarity index
Neighborhood disparities	Improvements in low-income and segregated neighborhoods on key measures of neighborhood opportunity, such as school performance, crime, and transportation access	Reduced disparities between neighborhoods in key measures of opportunity, such as school performance, crime, and transportation access

[a] Cities also may wish to track the extent to which people of different income levels can afford to live in the city more generally. The focus here is on the affordability of housing in resource-rich areas because that is the housing measure most relevant to economic mobility efforts, but the broader measure has value for measuring progress toward greater inclusion. Given the challenges that moderate-income working households in many cities are experiencing in affording housing, it would be worthwhile to focus this measure on a range of different income bands, including 0 to 30 percent of area median income (AMI), 30 to 50 percent of AMI, 50 to 80 percent of AMI, and 80 to 120 percent of AMI.

There are many different ways to measure these outcomes, and this book does not mean to suggest that the measures included here are the only or even the best ways to do so. Rather, illustrative measures are included to show that progress can be measured using publicly available data, as well as to offer suggestions for directions cities may want to consider in measuring progress. Ultimately, cities should select the measures that work best for capturing the progress toward achieving their goals.

The appendix provides an overview of the approaches summarized in figure 3. These measures by no means represent an exhaustive list of possible approaches, but they should provide enough information to show that such measurement is possible and to suggest a broad direction for cities to consider. These measures should also help clarify the kinds of outcomes that can be expected from efforts to promote economic mobility.

To be sure, many forces affecting these outcomes are beyond city control, such as macroeconomic influences like inflation and recession. Also, cities at times will make material and measurable progress that is too small to be reflected in their aggregate data. These caveats are important but do not constitute valid reasons for failing to measure whether progress is being made. Even if initial progress is too small to show up in data, a city's persistence in chipping away at these problems will eventually yield results. And the act of regularly measuring and publishing results may provide a powerful reminder of the persistence of challenges and bolster a city's motivation to act at the scale needed to achieve results that are larger and have greater impact.

CHAPTER 3

Place-Based Strategies

IN HIS WEEKLY RADIO ADDRESS on July 11, 2015, President Barack Obama summed up the problem meant to be addressed by place-based strategies promoting economic mobility.

> In some cities, kids living just blocks apart lead incredibly different lives. They go to different schools, play in different parks, shop in different stores, and walk down different streets. And often, the quality of those schools and the safety of those parks and streets are far from equal—which means those kids aren't getting an equal shot in life.
>
> That runs against the values we hold dear as Americans. In this country, of all countries, a person's zip code shouldn't decide their destiny. We don't guarantee equal outcomes, but we do strive to guarantee an equal shot at opportunity—in every neighborhood, for every American.

The former president's statement makes the case clearly for improving education, safety, and other services in the communities where low- and moderate-income families live. Providing these services in communities that need them is one of two key ways that place-based strategies can help individuals realize their economic potential.

But as fair housing advocates remind us, focusing only on strengthening low-income communities is not sufficient. It may take many years to improve a neighborhood, and some efforts will be unsuccessful. In the meantime, children will grow up attending low-quality schools and living in unsafe neighborhoods, lowering their educational achievement and earnings potential as adults. African American and Latino children will be more likely than other children to experience these challenges, violating the basic notions of fairness and the rights guaranteed by the Fair Housing Act of 1968.

To ensure that everyone has equitable access to the place-based resources that promote economic mobility, low- and moderate-income households need real and meaningful choices about where to live. This can be accomplished only by ensuring that affordable housing is available throughout a city, including and especially in areas that provide the building blocks of economic mobility, such as high-performing schools, public transportation, and safe streets. This is the second way that place-based strategies can help individuals moved up the economic ladder.

These two approaches are sometimes described as alternatives, with advocates and practitioners urging an emphasis on one approach or the other. This is surely a false choice: cities need to do both! It would be unfair to focus a city's resources on expanding affordable housing in areas that already provide the critical amenities associated with opportunity (henceforth termed *resource-rich areas*)[1] without also working to improve the quality of life for the majority of low- and moderate-income households, who live in low-income neighborhoods.

Though both components are necessary, neither is easy to achieve. Many resource-rich areas are largely built out and land prices can be very high, making it difficult to develop affordable housing. Land can be acquired and redeveloped more readily in struggling neighborhoods, but the challenges these neighborhoods face are complicated and multifaceted, requiring coordinated action across multiple policy domains. These challenges are emphasized here not to discourage action, but to underscore why it is so important for cities to step up and meet them head-on. They will only grow worse if neglected. To ensure that all residents have access to place-based resources, cities need to adopt a multifaceted strategy and invest energy and money in order to execute it with excellence.

This chapter reviews some of the many successful efforts cities have undertaken to ensure that place-based resources are provided. These examples show that cities can make substantial progress in addressing spatial inequities and provide lessons that can help other cities make faster progress. Addressed first—in the section "Reducing Neighborhood Disparities in Access to Opportunity"—are strategies for improving public services and amenities in low-income communities. Reviewed next—in the section "Increasing the Availability of Affordable Housing in Resource-Rich Areas"—are strategies for preserving and expanding affordable housing in areas providing the building blocks for economic mobility.

Before the case studies and policy recommendations that comprise the majority of this book are presented, key contexts in which this work takes place are briefly reviewed. These contexts are important for a range of reasons, but fundamentally because cities need to think strategically about place-based policies to promote economic mobility. Rather than view individual policies as standalone responses to disconnected challenges, cities should develop broader strategies that provide a comprehensive response to the underlying challenges.

Four Key Contexts for Place-Based Strategies

The first two contexts discussed here—the views of city residents and data on conditions in the city and individual neighborhoods—are important inputs for the development of a city's place-based strategy. The other contexts—a city's overall housing strategy and the HUD-required Assessment of Fair Housing—are broader plans into which place-based strategies for promoting economic mobility may fit.

UNDERSTANDING THE NEEDS AND VIEWS OF RESIDENTS

It almost goes without saying that city policies should be responsive to the views of city residents. Who would not agree with this goal? But it is emphasized here because of the fundamental importance of community input to the achievement of a more equitable society. The overriding goal of the efforts described in this book is to ensure that individuals and populations that have been left behind have the opportunity to advance economically. To accomplish this goal, it is critical to start with an understanding of the needs and views of these disenfranchised people. Local policy makers may have broad theories about what would make a difference in residents' lives, but they will not know for sure whether these theories reflect the reality until they reach out to residents and learn what they want. What are their aspirations for the future? What challenges are they experiencing? What are their priorities?

It is important to consider the views of *all* residents—and to this end, cities should explore the potential of technology to broaden the opportunity to gather input. (Some promising strategies in this area are discussed in chapter 5.) It is particularly important to understand the views of populations that are struggling to achieve economic mobility—including people of color, low-income residents, people with disabilities, and others—and of residents of neighborhoods that experience particularly tough challenges in such areas as education, crime, and access to jobs.

UNDERSTANDING NEIGHBORHOOD AND CITY CONDITIONS

The second essential input for development of a city's strategy is an understanding of basic data on conditions in specific neighborhoods as well as the city as a whole. The fundamental challenge that place-based efforts seek to address is spatial inequity—the fact that conditions in some neighborhoods are more supportive of individuals and families than those in other neighborhoods.

A key first step toward addressing these inequities is to understand them better. This involves a review of neighborhood conditions and a comparison across neighborhoods to identify which are struggling and in what way. This assessment can inform and help the city prioritize efforts to reduce neighborhood disparities. The review of neighborhood conditions also can help the city identify neighborhoods that are the strongest in the elements most important to child and adult well-being—an assessment that can help it identify the resource-rich neighborhoods it may want to prioritize for expansion of affordable housing.

Data on neighborhood-level measures are available from a number of sources, including HUD's Affirmatively Furthering Fair Housing database (https://egis.hud.gov/affht), the Diversity Data Kids project (www.Diversitydatakids.org), the Kirwan Institute for the Study of Race and Ethnicity at Ohio State University (http://kirwaninstitute. osu.edu), the National Equity Atlas (http://nationalequityatlas.org), and Enterprise Community Partners (www.enterprisecommunity.org/ research-and-resources). Local academic institutions can be an important source of assistance in reviewing and analyzing the data. One model of such a partnership is the report on New York City neighborhoods prepared annually by the New York University (NYU) Furman Center (http://furmancenter.org/research/sonychan).

Another model is to gather data directly from the public. The Motor City Mapping project (https://www.motorcitymapping.org), for example, engaged 150 Detroit residents to map the condition of blighted properties throughout the city, using the data to inform a report on the subject and to populate interactive maps that feed information back to the public. A similar approach is being used in Cleveland, Cincinnati, and Columbus (www.3csmapping.com). These approaches not only gather valuable information, but also involve the public, increasing resident engagement and understanding.

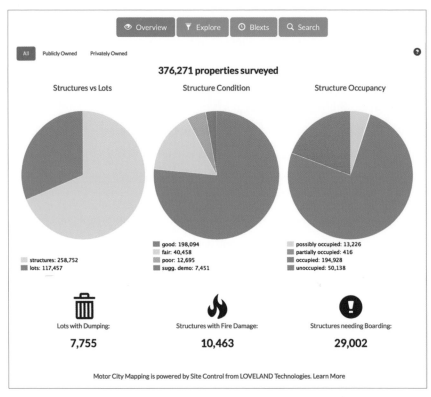

The Motor City Mapping project provides online property-condition data for more than 380,000 parcels in Detroit. *Motor City Mapping and Loveland Technologies*

In addition to data collection, cities will need to consider how to define a "resource-rich area"—that is, to determine which neighborhoods a city should target with efforts to increase the availability of affordable housing. Different localities have approached this question in different ways. Recommendations on how to approach the question follow.

- **BE FLEXIBLE IN HOW PROGRAMS AND POLICIES ARE APPLIED.**
  Though it is important to make informed decisions about which areas to target for affordable housing, the same definitions need not necessarily be applied to all programs and policies. For example, in developing a program to help households with Housing Choice Vouchers move to neighborhoods of opportunity, a city might adopt one definition—

focusing on school performance, poverty rate, or racial/ethnic composition—while simultaneously working to expand dedicated affordable housing in new and gentrifying neighborhoods not currently meeting this definition but likely to offer improving amenities over time.

- **USE LOCAL DATA WHERE POSSIBLE TO DIRECTLY MEASURE OPPORTUNITY FACTORS.** Historically, efforts to define "opportunity areas" (or as termed here, resource-rich areas) relied on proxies for opportunity, such as the poverty rate, at least in part because those data were the most readily available. With the improved availability of local administrative data—on school quality, transportation routes, blight, and crime—communities can now look more directly at indicators of opportunity to make more nuanced and informed determinations regarding where housing affordability efforts should be targeted. (See sidebar, following page.)

- **REMEMBER NEWER AND GENTRIFYING AREAS.** In many cases, efforts to help low-income households gain access to resource-rich areas have focused on fully built-out suburban areas. There is a good reason for this: such neighborhoods often have the strongest schools. But it is important not to overlook opportunities to embed affordable housing in newly developed subdivisions and in infill settings undergoing redevelopment and gentrification. In many cases, these areas will see amenities and services improve over time, becoming resource rich. It is also significantly easier—and often less expensive—to incorporate affordability into development taking place in these areas.

Illustrative Definitions of Resource-Rich Areas

SEVERAL PROGRAMS AROUND THE UNITED STATES have developed a definition of opportunity- or resource-rich areas as part of their effort to identify locations in which to increase the availability of affordable housing.

■ **KING COUNTY, WASHINGTON.** As part of its Moving to Work program, the King County Housing Authority (KCHA) has established a goal to "increase housing choices in high-opportunity neighborhoods."[2] KCHA identifies these resource-rich areas using 20 indicators developed by the Puget Sound Regional Council, a metropolitan planning organization for the Puget Sound area, and the Kirwan Institute. The indicators are divided into five categories: education, including measures of student performance and teacher qualification; economic health, which focuses mainly on employment; housing and neighborhood quality, including vacancy and foreclosure rates; mobility and transportation, which looks at transportation costs and access; and health and environment, which assesses both proximity to neighborhood assets and environmental hazards.[3]

■ **DALLAS, TEXAS.** Families with a Housing Choice Voucher from the Dallas Housing Authority may be eligible to participate in the Mobility Assistance Program, which provides an array of services to help them find housing in "high opportunity areas" (HOAs). HOAs are census tracts that meet the terms established in the settlement of a class-action lawsuit, *Walker v. HUD*, plus a few additional criteria. Specifically, HOA census tracts must have poverty rates at or below 10 percent and household incomes at or above 80 percent of the area median income. The percentage of African American residents must be 25.7 percent or below, and there can be no public housing units. Finally, public schools in HOAs must be "high performing," meaning the neighborhood elementary school for the address has been rated as "met stan-

COMPREHENSIVE LOCAL HOUSING STRATEGIES

The third context for a city's place-based efforts is its broader housing strategy. Though cities are not required to develop a comprehensive local housing strategy, it is generally valuable to do so. Because cities generally seek to achieve multiple housing policy objectives simultaneously,[4] their

dards" by the Texas Education Agency and the high school has a four-year graduation rate of at least 85 percent.[5]

■ **CHICAGO, ILLINOIS.** Through the Chicago Regional Housing Choice Initiative, ten public housing agencies in and around Chicago have created a virtual pool of project-based vouchers (a type of HUD rental assistance subsidy) that are available on a competitive basis for developments that meet regional priorities—among these, location in an "opportunity area." The participating housing agencies have established a shared definition of opportunity areas that is based on an opportunity index developed by HUD, with some adjustment for local conditions. To identify opportunity areas, census tracts are assessed according to six criteria—housing stability, job access, transit access, poverty, labor market engagement, and school performance— each of which is weighted equally to derive a score from 1 to 10. Census tracts with a score of 6 to 10 are considered opportunity areas. The initiative also supports developments in lower-ranking tracts if they are part of a broader revitalization strategy.

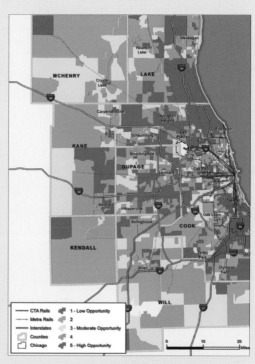

The Chicago Regional Housing Initiative defined and mapped indicators of opportunity at the census-tract level in the Chicago metro region as a basis for targeting its housing mobility and counseling efforts. Indicators include labor-market engagement, job access, transportation access, housing stability, poverty, and school performance. *Chicago Metropolitan Agency for Planning*

strategies likely will cover a broader array of policies than those focused solely or mainly on expanding the availability of affordable housing in resource-rich areas. A comprehensive local housing strategy provides cities with a framework for coordinating all their housing policies to achieve locally defined objectives.

There is a tendency in housing policy, as in other areas, to want to jump right in and start implementing promising practices. Though the enthusiasm and can-do spirit behind this impulse is admirable, one lesson learned from reviewing the successes and failures of local efforts to promote economic mobility and equity is the importance of a comprehensive approach that integrates a range of coordinated policies across multiple domains to achieve a common goal.

No one policy can single-handedly achieve the objective of preserving and expanding the availability of affordable housing in resource-rich areas, or any other objective of a city's housing policy, for that matter. Rather than look for a magic bullet, communities need to consider and ensure the coordination of multiple policies across different city departments and agencies. Having an overall strategy, documented in a publicly available plan, with associated goals that can be measured over time, is important for ensuring that communities can activate and coordinate all the policies needed to achieve success.

To achieve the objective of preserving and expanding affordable housing in resource-rich areas—as well as other related housing policy objectives—communities should develop a comprehensive local housing strategy that (a) uses the full range of tools at the disposal of local government, and (b) engages the private and nonprofit sectors as partners in working to achieve common objectives.

A comprehensive local housing strategy differs from the numerous housing-related plans required by federal (and in some cases state) government in three ways:

- It is focused on achieving locally defined policy objectives.
- It is inclusive of *all* the policy tools available to the local government.

- It is a product of dialogue and coordination across *all* the relevant local government departments, including, among others, departments of planning and zoning, housing and community development, taxation, and permitting, as well as the local public housing agencies and local housing finance agencies.

While no agreed-upon framework for developing a comprehensive local housing strategy currently exists, an effort is underway to develop one. This effort—the National Community of Practice on Local Housing Policy[6]—is bringing together a diverse group of experts from around the country to compile guidance on how cities and counties can develop stronger housing strategies. Informed by a broad-based advisory council of more than 40 organizations (including the Urban Land Institute), the Community of Practice is focused in particular on cities and counties in high-cost regions, but its efforts are relevant to any city or county that has high-cost neighborhoods. Though the final products of this effort will not be available until 2018, the latest draft of the policy framework has been used here to structure a review of housing policy options.

The Community of Practice has identified four core categories of local housing policies necessary for increasing housing affordability:

- creating and preserving dedicated affordable housing units;

- promoting affordability by increasing the overall supply of housing and lowering barriers and costs;

- helping renters and homebuyers gain access to and afford units they locate in the private market; and

- ensuring housing stability and quality.

In selecting policies for inclusion in their plans, cities should be guided by their core policy objectives as well as the resources available to them and their internal capacity. Larger jurisdictions in high-cost regions would be well served by adopting robust policies in all four of these categories. Smaller communities would also benefit from considering policies in all four areas, though because they have less capacity, they may need to rely more heavily on county and state government policies to supplement local policies. Jurisdictions outside high-cost regions may not view development of affordable housing as a priority given comparatively low median rents and sale prices. Even if housing is relatively affordable in the jurisdiction or region overall, however, rents and home prices in resource-rich neighborhoods may be out of reach of low-income households. If so, the policies discussed in this volume will be helpful.

The final section of this chapter, "Increasing the Availability of Affordable Housing in Resource-Rich Areas," reviews examples of specific policies in each of these four categories that can help preserve or expand the availability of affordable housing, illustrated by case studies showing the policies in action in specific communities. Due to the large number of policies that fall into the first category—creating and preserving dedicated affordable housing units—the focus in that section is first on that category alone, then on the remaining three categories together.

HUD-REQUIRED ASSESSMENT OF FAIR HOUSING

The final context addressed here is the HUD-required Assessment of Fair Housing (AFH). The place-based strategies described in this chapter overlap in important ways with the policies included in the AFH.

The AFH, the successor to the Analysis of Impediments to Fair Housing, is required of all recipients of funding from certain HUD housing programs, including the HOME and Community Development Block Grant programs in which most large cities participate. The legal mandate that motivates the AFH—the duty of HUD and its grantees to "affirmatively further fair housing"—requires cities to plan for how they will go beyond simple compliance with antidiscrimination laws to carry out that duty. Most jurisdictions are required to update their AFH plans every five years.

As defined by HUD in 24 CFR §5.152:

Affirmatively furthering fair housing means taking meaningful actions, in addition to combating discrimination, that
overcome patterns of segregation and foster inclusive communities free from barriers that restrict access to opportunity
based on protected characteristics. Specifically, affirmatively
furthering fair housing means taking meaningful actions
that, taken together, address significant disparities in housing
needs and in access to opportunity, replacing segregated living
patterns with truly integrated and balanced living patterns,
transforming racially and ethnically concentrated areas of
poverty into areas of opportunity, and fostering and main-
taining compliance with civil rights and fair housing laws.
The duty to affirmatively further fair housing extends to all
of a program participant's activities and programs relating to
housing and urban development.

As reflected in this definition, the duty to further fair housing—and
by extension the AFH that plans for how the jurisdiction will pursue
that duty—includes an explicit focus on addressing disparities in access
to the neighborhood-level resources that promote economic mobility.
HUD guidance makes it clear that this includes a focus both on increasing the availability of affordable housing in resource-rich areas
and on strengthening the opportunities available to racial and ethnic
minorities and other members of protected classes in their current
neighborhoods—a two-pronged approach similar to the two place-based
approaches addressed here. This means that the place-based efforts cities undertake to promote economic mobility will help them complete a
successful AFH and, conversely, that the AFH process should help cities
identify areas for improvement in those efforts.

While cities should strive to prepare excellent AFH plans, they should go beyond the minimum planning required by HUD to continually and actively plan for strengthening their approach to addressing spatial inequities. Rather than seeing the AFH as a substitute for these broader and ongoing planning efforts, cities should see the AFH process as an opportunity to periodically gather new data and input to refine and strengthen their approach. Among other benefits of the AFH process, cities will find that the data analysis and public consultation processes will provide valuable input to strengthen their place-based strategies.

Reducing Neighborhood Disparities in Access to Opportunity

Residents of all neighborhoods deserve the same opportunity to gain access to the critical amenities associated with economic opportunity. At a minimum, this includes high-quality public schools, safe streets, and good transportation access to jobs. More broadly, cities should strive to address other neighborhood-level disparities as well, including those in health outcomes and in access to parks and other open space, sports and cultural activities, and fresh fruits and vegetables.

Four place-based approaches to addressing neighborhood-level disparities are addressed here. By necessity, this list is illustrative rather than exhaustive.

- **COMPREHENSIVE COMMUNITY DEVELOPMENT**—an approach to neighborhood revitalization that involves addressing multiple challenges simultaneously in order to achieve the scale of change necessary to alter a neighborhood's trajectory.

- **COMMUNITY DEVELOPMENT SPURRED BY ANCHOR INSTITUTIONS**—an alternative approach that relies heavily on coordinated activities by one or more anchor institutions, such as a hospital or university.

- **COMMUNITY BENEFITS AGREEMENTS**—a way of leveraging large-scale private development to generate benefits for local residents. Execution of these agreements requires the community to be well organized enough to ask for reasonably achievable public benefits as a quid pro quo for the developer benefits that may be needed to allow the development to proceed.

- **REDUCING DISPARITIES IN EDUCATION OUTCOMES BY NEIGH-BORHOOD, INCOME, RACE, AND ETHNICITY**—a systemwide strategy in which a city-level agency reduces neighborhood disparities by allocating resources and oversight in a manner designed to ensure that all schools meet the district's standards for a high-quality education.

DEVELOPMENT OF AN OVERALL STRATEGY FOR REDUCING NEIGHBORHOOD DISPARITIES

As with the development of affordable housing strategies, there is merit in thinking comprehensively and strategically about approaches for reducing neighborhood disparities. This has both a neighborhood-level dimension, because each neighborhood faces unique challenges, and a citywide dimension, because city agencies control the allocation of many resources, including those for schools, public safety, and parks and recreation.

One important step is to thoroughly understand the assets and challenges of each neighborhood. Each neighborhood has a unique history, demographics, and set of public buildings and parks. By understanding these features and the aspirations of residents for the development of their neighborhood, cities can develop customized plans for strengthening each neighborhood that builds on its assets and addresses its challenges.

At the same time, cities need to consider how resources are allocated across neighborhoods. A city generally has a single school system, a single oversight body for public parks, and a single police department responsible for public safety. With limited resources available, cities need to decide how to allocate those resources so as to meet the needs of residents of each neighborhood. Neighborhoods that have been short-changed—as reflected, for example, in older schools that are physically deteriorating and offering classes with below-average teachers, or in parks that are poorly maintained compared with parks in other neighborhoods—deserve their fair share of the resources. Such neighborhoods may even need more resources than others to make up for historical deficiencies in allocations or to address more profound challenges.

Many struggling neighborhoods experience multiple challenges at the same time, including low-quality schools, unsafe streets, a lack of retailers and private investment, poor transportation access to job centers, and high rates of poverty and segregation. In such circumstances, experience has shown that interventions focused on improving only one service or amenity often fail to change the community dynamic or produce lasting change. For this reason, many cities seek to work simultaneously on strengthening multiple components of the community fabric and thereby generate more comprehensive and durable change.

Ideally, then, cities should have individual plans for neighborhoods that focus on comprehensively addressing the challenges each faces, as well as citywide efforts to more equitably allocate city resources to reduce neighborhood disparities. In this chapter, examples are provided of both neighborhood-specific efforts and systemwide efforts to reduce neighborhood disparities.

COMPREHENSIVE COMMUNITY DEVELOPMENT

Comprehensive community development initiatives focus simultaneously on strengthening two or more aspects of a neighborhood in order to exert the kinds of large, concentrated effects that many believe are needed to change a community's trajectory. For example, such an initiative may seek to combine improvements in local schools with improvements in public safety, expanded job training programs, and support for development of resident-owned businesses. When successful, such initiatives help address neighborhood disparities both by improving the services and amenities available in a community—for example, through the development of a new school and implementation of coordinated supports for student achievement—and by altering the trajectory of a neighborhood in ways that pave the way for increased private investment and racial and ethnic integration.

As one report defines the term, comprehensive community development initiatives tend to be characterized by the following attributes:

- they are broad-based collaborations of service providers, residents, advocates, businesses, governments, and other stakeholders that come together to develop comprehensive and integrated multilevel service and policy responses to poverty;

- they are community-based, meaning both located in specific places and contexts, and being driven by community needs, perspectives, and mobilization;

- they have long time horizons and broad ambitions—working to mobilize local communities to transform the conditions and constraints that underlie poverty.[7]

These points should be thought of as elements with which to describe and assess comprehensive community development initiatives rather than as a rigid definition. Though all such initiatives necessarily involve multifaceted efforts to strengthen a neighborhood, not all grow organically out of the actions of local residents or community organizers. Similarly, not all such efforts will be equally comprehensive in terms of the number and magnitude of the community development activities being implemented and the number and range of local collaborators.

While comprehensive community development initiatives are often spearheaded by local community development corporations— neighborhood-based nonprofit organizations established to strengthen communities—they can also be initiated by institutional actors, such as local schools, public housing agencies, philanthropic institutions, or city community development departments. The federal government has supported a number of comprehensive community development efforts, including the Choice Neighborhoods and Promise Neighborhoods programs. The Choice Neighborhoods program uses the revitalization of a distressed public or assisted housing development to anchor a broader set of efforts to strengthen a community. The Promise Neighborhoods

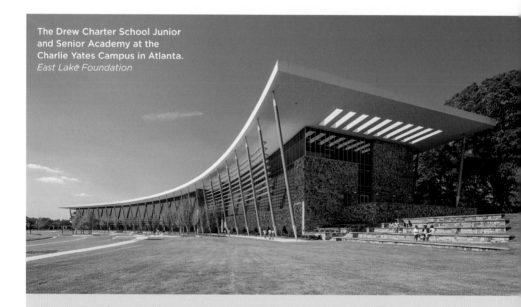

The Drew Charter School Junior and Senior Academy at the Charlie Yates Campus in Atlanta.
East Lake Foundation

COMPREHENSIVE COMMUNITY DEVELOPMENT

Centennial Place and East Lake, Atlanta, Georgia

Holistic efforts integrating real estate development, school reform, and community wellness transform entire neighborhoods.

ATLANTA'S RAPID RISE to the ranks of world-class cities was solidified for many by its selection in 1990 to host the 1996 Summer Olympics. Hidden from most outsiders, though vivid to a growing number of Atlantans, were worsening problems of crime and concentrated poverty in the city's larg-

program takes a similar approach but anchors its revitalization efforts on the strengthening of local schools and education services.

The Centennial Place and East Lake case study illustrates elements of both approaches by combining the revitalization of distressed public housing with the construction of new schools to create change of sufficient scale to alter the neighborhood's trajectory. The case study focuses on two redevelopment efforts undertaken by the Atlanta Housing Authority—one with a grant from the HOPE VI program, the predecessor of

est public housing communities, some of which were located in and around where the city planned major redevelopment to accommodate the Games.

One example was Techwood and Clark Howell Homes, adjacent public housing projects that had opened in 1936 and 1941, respectively. These projects had more than 1,100 units on 60 acres located just west of the central business district and across the street from the proposed site of the Olympic dormitories. It had been agreed in 1992 that the Atlanta Housing Authority (AHA) would sell two acres to the Georgia Board of Regents for that purpose. The Olympic dormitories would later be retrofitted and sold to Georgia State University for use as student housing.

Nine of ten of Techwood/Clark Howell residents lived in poverty and only 18 percent were employed. Annual wages averaged less than $5,000 per year. The violent crime rate at the projects was 69 percent higher than the average for the city overall. The neighborhood's Fowler Elementary School ranked 60th among 71 city public schools.[8]

East Lake Meadows, which opened in 1970, was in a similar or worse condition. The surrounding area had a 96 percent poverty rate and an average resident income under $5,000. Ninety percent of the 1,400 residents had been victims of a crime. Only 5 percent of the fifth-grade students at the Drew Elementary School were meeting state math standards, and less than 30 percent of neighborhood students were graduating from high school.[9]

In the early 1990s, Atlanta, which had suffered from the flight of upper- and middle-income white and African American families, was the second-poorest city in the nation, behind only Newark, New Jersey.

→

Equity Strategies, Results, and Challenges

After a successful career in corporate law and finance, Renée Lewis Glover in 1994 became executive director of the AHA, the agency that owned and operated Techwood and Clark Howell Homes, and East Lake Meadows. Glover and Dr. Norman Johnson of the Georgia Institute of Technology, who was also a member of Atlanta Board of Education, were heartbroken to learn that no child, white or black, who lived in Techwood Homes during its 60-year history had ever crossed the street to attend Georgia Tech.[10]

The holistic transformation of Techwood/Clark Howell Homes—by a public/ private partnership that included AHA and developers the Integral Group and McCormack Baron Salazar—into Centennial Place constituted the first mixed-income, mixed-use community in the United States with public housing–assisted units as a component.

Egbert Perry of the Integral Group and Richard Baron of McCormack Baron Salazar—collectively, the Integral Partnership of Atlanta (TIPA)—and Glover understood that in order to create a mixed-income development, the master plan for the communities had to offer high-quality housing and quality-of-life amenities that would attract and retain upper- and middle-class families who could choose to live where they wanted. The most important consideration was the quality of the neighborhood schools.

Centennial Place has 738 mixed-income rental apartments, with 40 percent market rate, 40 percent assisted by AHA, and 20 percent affordable to moderate-income households. Centennial Place Elementary School, which opened in 1998 with commitments from the Atlanta Public Schools to operate independently, has earned outstanding academic results, climbing to rank among the five highest-performing schools in the state. It became the first school in Atlanta to adopt an extended school day and a year-round calendar.

A researcher recently observed that while the school "no longer leads the state in academic achievement, [it] seems to do reasonably well. . . . The students are still mostly African American and mostly come from low-income families, but there are middle-class students, as well as white and Asian students. It is, apparently, beginning to attract the university community to send its children to the school, which was unthinkable years ago."[11]

The neighborhood around Centennial Place is also safer and has attracted more than $500 million in new investment, including new housing. Analysts from the Urban Institute concluded that at least three-quarters of the new housing in the neighborhood would not have been developed if the previous public housing developments had remained.[12]

Locally based developer Tom Cousins pursued a similar path after learning that East Lake Meadows was one of the major feeders of the Georgia prison system. Working with the residents and representatives of the Cousins Foundation, AHA, with TIPA as its program manager, razed East Lake Meadows. After concluding the procurement process, AHA partnered with the East Lake Foundation to redevelop the site as a mixed-income, mixed-use community with 542 units of new garden apartments, townhouses, and villas divided equally between market-rate and affordable housing.

The East Lake Foundation, established by Cousins to complement his development efforts, then led the approval for and development of Atlanta's first public charter school, the Charles R. Drew School, which saw 98 percent of its students in grades three through eight meet or exceed state standards in 2012–2013. Drew Senior Academy, a high school, was added in 2014 with a freshman class of 100 students. The East Lake elementary and middle schools added an hour and a half to the school day and extended the school year by five days. Drew Senior Academy adopted the same program and, judged by recent test scores of the students admitted, is on track to be as successful as the school's lower grades.

Today, the Villages of East Lake is a mixed-income community of 1,500 where residences are evenly divided between affordable and market-rate units. As a result of redevelopment, the area has attracted more than $175 million in new investment. Home values have risen at a rate almost four times faster than that for Atlanta as a whole, a sign that the marketplace recognizes the improved quality of life in the neighborhood.

Fully 70 percent of East Lake's public housing residents today are either employed or enrolled in education or job-training programs. Crime overall has declined by 73 percent and violent crime by 90 percent. The neighborhood now has a crime rate half that of Atlanta overall.[13]

the Choice Neighborhoods program, and the second with the assistance of a local philanthropist. Together, these examples highlight the potential of comprehensive community development efforts to strengthen local neighborhoods in ways that lead to improvements in school quality, a reduction in crime, and the fostering of mixed-income communities.

Though successful in many ways in revitalizing distressed public housing communities, the HOPE VI program (like other redevelopment efforts) has been criticized for not providing enough support for longtime residents, many of whom move to another location using Housing Choice Vouchers rather than return to the redeveloped site. A strong focus on equity throughout the process can help such programs preemptively address these concerns. Promising approaches include working closely with residents to understand their concerns and aspirations for the redeveloped community, helping existing residents identify and gain access to housing options of their choice in resource-rich areas, and ensuring that residents who want to return have a viable path to do so.

COMMUNITY DEVELOPMENT SPURRED BY ANCHOR INSTITUTIONS

Another approach to revitalizing struggling neighborhoods is to build on the assets provided by large anchor institutions, such as hospitals or universities, that may already be operating in the neighborhood. In West Philadelphia, for example, a long-term partnership among the University of Pennsylvania, the city, and neighborhood organizations and businesses led to the injection of millions of dollars into the local economy as the university committed to purchasing a share of its products and services from local businesses.[14] Among other things, anchor institutions can provide jobs, internships, and apprenticeship opportunities; strengthen local schools; provide volunteers to build homes and deliver necessary services; support public safety and neighborhood beautification; and contribute in numerous other ways to community development objectives.

The key is for the anchor institutions to understand the mutual benefits of partnering with the city and neighborhood organizations to leverage the anchor's day-to-day activities to improve the neighborhood's quality of life. Historically, as the neighborhoods in which they were located began to change, many anchor institutions turned inward, focusing on their own well-being despite the challenges faced by neighborhood residents. In recent decades, however, a growing number of success stories has helped universities, hospitals, museums, and large businesses understand that modest reconfigurations of their business processes can simultaneously improve the quality of life for residents and their own employees.

The Greater University Circle Initiative case study focuses on how the partnership among the Cleveland Foundation and large institutions in Cleveland's University Circle neighborhood use the collective buying power of these institutions to create jobs for area residents and support local businesses. The city has supported revitalization of the area by investing more than $100 million in the Cleveland Health-Tech Corridor to support brownfield and environmental remediation, beautification, and construction and rehabilitation of properties.

COMMUNITY BENEFITS AGREEMENTS

As the Greater University Circle Initiative illustrates, public investment is not the only way that struggling communities acquire more amenities. Private investment also plays an important role. For example, when residential property owners invest in their properties, they may attract residents with moderate incomes to live in the neighborhood who in turn have the spending power to support restaurants and specialty retail stores. Those businesses devote those receipts in part to commercial investments that in turn may further enhance the desirability of the neighborhood and attract other residents who can help bring energy and enthusiasm to local schools and neighborhood volunteer efforts.

Greater University Circle Initiative, Cleveland, Ohio

World-class health and education institutions and a local government commit to expanding neighborhood businesses, community jobs, and resident wealth in the inner city.

CLEVELAND'S UNIVERSITY CIRCLE neighborhood on the city's east side is renowned for its concentration of world-class education, medical, and arts institutions. They include the Cleveland Clinic, University Hospitals, Case Western Reserve University, the Cleveland Orchestra, and the Cleveland Museum of Art. The area is an economic powerhouse for the city and region, providing nearly 30,000 jobs and attracting 2.5 million visitors a year.

Employees of Evergreen Energy Solutions install solar panels on the roof of a University Hospital building in Cleveland. *Cleveland Foundation*

Despite these economic assets, much of the area around University Circle has long been characterized by high levels of unemployment and poverty and persistent racial and economic segregation. Historically, little of the $3 billion in annual direct spending by the neighborhood's anchor institutions has created jobs for the area's low-income residents or generated opportunities for neighborhood businesses. When Ron Richard became president and chief executive officer of the Cleveland Foundation in 2003 after a long career in business and government, he perceived an "invisible divide" that was separating University Circle's institutions and its community—and hurting both.[15]

Over the past 15 years, the Cleveland Foundation has worked with the community, the institutions, the city of Cleveland, and corporate and public sector partners to bridge that divide. Much of the initiative has focused on physical redevelopment of the area, following the example of successful anchor-led initiatives by the University of Pennsylvania in Philadelphia and Ohio State University in Columbus during the 1990s and early 2000s. The Cleveland effort has also broken new ground in focusing with equal intensity and innovation on expanding community and resident financial assets. "Our goal is equitable wealth creation at scale," Richard said.[16]

Equity Strategies, Results, and Challenges

While Cleveland's leaders were inspired by the success of anchor-led efforts elsewhere, they determined that a new model was needed to fully unleash the potential in and, particularly, around University Circle.

First, theirs would be a *multi-anchor* strategy in which no single institution was the central driver. The equal partners are BioEnterprise, Case Western Reserve University, the city of Cleveland, Cleveland Clinic, Cleveland Foundation, Cleveland State University, Greater Cleveland Regional Transit Authority, Kelvin and Eleanor Smith Foundation, Kent H. Smith Charitable Trust, Neighborhood Connections, Neighborhood Progress Inc., University Circle Inc., and University Hospitals.

Second, the revitalization effort, the Greater University Circle Initiative, would build outward from University Circle to also address the needs of the surrounding neighborhoods—Hough, Glenville, East Cleveland, Little Italy, Buckeye/Shaker, Fairfax, and Central. The Cleveland Foundation would act as the hub and coordinator of each institution's related efforts, serving as an honest broker and providing seed funding for catalytic projects.

Much of the initiative's real estate and economic development activities are focused on the Cleveland Health-Tech Corridor—running about three miles from downtown Cleveland through University Circle and into East Cleveland—and 1,600 acres around this corridor. Over the past decade, the city has invested more than $100 million in the corridor, generating more than a half billion dollars in construction, rehabilitation, remediation, and beautification efforts. Other anchor partners have worked to attract and retain companies, with significant success.[17]

In 2015, University Hospitals announced plans to move its women's and children's primary care clinic to the area. The NewBridge Cleveland Center for Arts & Technology, located in the corridor, trains unemployed and underemployed adults for careers in health care. From 2011 through 2016, 318 people enrolled in the training programs, 225 graduated, and 142 found jobs.

The Greater University Circle Initiative is also working to attract anchor-institution employees to live in the area. Greater Circle Living, an initiative-sponsored program offering employee housing assistance, provides forgivable loans, matching funds for exterior renovations, and a month's rent to participating employees. The program provided $4.4 million of incentives between 2008 and 2016 to 368 anchor-institution employees. These incentives have leveraged an additional $30.2 million in Greater University Circle through home purchase, home improvement, and rental assistance programs.[18]

Another element of the equitable wealth strategy has been the fostering of the Evergreen Cooperatives, a network of employee-owned small businesses launched in 2007. Between 2009 and 2013, three Evergreen businesses opened: the Evergreen Cooperative Laundry, which serves hotels, hospitals, and nursing homes, using environmentally friendly cleaning practices; Evergreen Energy Solutions, which installs renewable energy systems and makes energy efficiency improvements to buildings; and Green City Growers, which supplies sustainably grown vegetables and herbs to grocers and restaurants throughout northeast Ohio.

As of the end of 2016, all three businesses were still operating and employed a total of 113 people. The average hourly wage of the three businesses is about $14.[19] All employees of the three ventures are minorities, and 47 percent are people returning from incarceration.[20] The laundry and energy services company began sharing profits with employees in 2013, and Green City Growers was approaching profitability at the end of 2016.[21]

This idealized picture is complicated by both the fears and reality of neighborhood change. Though such change sometimes happens gradually in ways that benefit longtime residents, it also can happen quickly in ways that lead to the displacement of those residents. The biggest fears tend to be associated with the biggest projects—construction of a new sports arena, for example, or the comprehensive development of a large tract of publicly owned land. Residents worry that these larger projects will have a big impact on their neighborhood, leading to higher rents and retail prices and increased traffic, as well as their own displacement.

Often in such cases the development is carried out through a public/private partnership. The public investment could be in the form of tax breaks for a new stadium; construction of the roads, sidewalks, sewers, and other infrastructure needed for the new development; a discount on the price of public land; or simply a change in the zoning rules to accommodate the new development.

In these cases, residents and their advocates often argue that the public should get something in return for its investment. In particular, they argue that the development should provide benefits for neighborhood residents to compensate for the disproportionate effects the development will have on them. For example, the development of a stadium could lead to an increase in the value of surrounding properties, which in turn pushes up rents and may lead some residential property owners to reposition a property as a restaurant or other business serving the people arriving at the stadium. The broader community may see the new restaurant or business as an important city amenity, but the residents who were living in the building before the change may find themselves displaced and without the ability to find alternative neighborhood housing they can afford.

This line of argument has led to the development of community benefits agreements designed to ensure that private development facilitated by public subsidies or other public contributions provides concrete benefits to the neighborhoods and people most affected by that development. The community benefits included in such agreements may include, for example, jobs for local residents associated with the construction or operation of the new development; development of affordable housing; and parks and other recreational facilities for neighborhood residents. Though community benefits agreements often have been triggered by protests by neighborhood residents and community organizing by local advocates, they also can be negotiated directly by cities seeking to maximize the benefits associated with new development and to offset any harm to the immediate neighborhood.

Equity Strategies, Results, and Challenges

With emergence of the redevelopment opportunity, the Good Jobs and Livable Neighborhoods Coalition was formed to advocate a set of community benefits in connection with the Park East redevelopment. The coalition—made up of the Milwaukee County Labor Council, the Institute for Wisconsin's Future, a coalition of churches called Milwaukee Inner-City Congregations Allied for Hope, and other faith-based and labor groups—set several priorities: payment of prevailing wages for construction workers, training and job opportunities for area residents, funding and development of affordable housing, and use of environmentally sustainable construction practices.

The coalition was unable to persuade Milwaukee's mayor and city council to include its priorities in the final redevelopment agreement adopted in 2004; according to one assessment of the campaign, the council and mayor opposed the community benefits package out of "concern that the provisions being sought would inflate construction costs and doubts about the legality of setting housing and workforce policy in a land use document."[26]

However, 16 acres of the site were owned by Milwaukee County, which did adopt most of the community benefits program in 2005. Under the Park East Redevelopment Compact (PERC), proposals from developers seeking to build on county-controlled land are evaluated according to the extent to which they "will provide the greatest future benefit in jobs, tax base, and image for the community, as well as a fair price."[27] Projects also must meet green building criteria. In addition, the compact calls on Milwaukee County to sponsor new affordable housing amounting to no less than 20 percent of the housing units built on Park East land (although the units may be built off site).

The PERC also requires developers to provide apprenticeship programs and training opportunities to help low-income, low-skilled residents qualify for construction positions, and businesses locating in the development area are required, whenever possible, to be locally owned and pay "living wages." In addition, at least 25 percent of the construction jobs must be from businesses designated as disadvantaged business enterprises or minority business enterprises, and 5 percent must be businesses designated as women's business enterprises. A community oversight board exists to monitor construction and subsequent development and ensure that all parties abide by the PERC.

With a community benefits agreement finally in place, the next challenge was the Great Recession, which stalled redevelopment of the area for several years. Progress has been substantial since the economic recovery, though. Since 2011, developments have been proposed or completed on 98 percent of the county-owned portion of the redevelopment area.[28] In 2014, the county awarded the ownership group of the Milwaukee Bucks NBA team the rights to develop a ten-acre parcel as the site of a $524 million arena, parking structure, and training facility/health center. The Bucks also announced plans for additional mixed-use development in the rest of the Park East corridor.

The arena agreement was controversial and negotiations were contentious, as real estate transactions between sports teams and cities often are. Yet the commitment to community benefits is significant and builds on the efforts of community leaders and county officials through the PERC.

The Bucks and the Alliance for Good Jobs, a local advocacy group, pledged to create a first-source hiring program that will require at least half of covered employees in the arena district to reside (at the time of hire) in economically distressed Milwaukee zip codes. In addition, covered employees of the new arena and in the surrounding area will be paid at least $15 per hour by 2023, rising from $12 per hour in 2017. Under the agreement, arena-area employees will have "an opportunity to unionize in an environment that is neutral and free from traditional pressures" associated with some labor-organizing efforts.[29]

Said the lead negotiator for the Alliance for Good Jobs, "This agreement establishes a community standard for living wages, workers' rights, and access to good jobs that should be applied to every new development, to every institution in our community, to all the other employers in this town so that we take those service-sector jobs that are trapping people in poverty and help them become the bedrock of the middle class."[30]

REDUCING DISPARITIES IN EDUCATION OUTCOMES BY NEIGHBORHOOD, INCOME, RACE, AND ETHNICITY

Many neighborhood disparities affect the opportunities available to local residents, but disparities in the quality of public schools are of particular concern. There simply is no reason why a child living in a neighborhood characterized by poverty or racial or ethnic segregation should receive a lower-quality education than a child in another neighborhood. Children who grow up in neighborhoods with low-quality schools are less likely to be employed or go to college than those in other neighborhoods.[31] Early childhood is the best time to intervene to change the trajectory of a person's life and help improve that individual's opportunities.[32]

It is an indication of the importance of public education that it can be addressed as either a place-based or people-based strategy. A place-based approach is important because frequently inequities exist in the quality of education between one local school and the next. At the same time, a people-based perspective is important because in many school districts there is a need to boost the quality of public education for everyone, and the entire system needs to function effectively to meet the needs of all children.

The focus in this chapter is on place-based improvements to public schools that help narrow gaps according to neighborhood, race, and ethnicity. In cities where schools are neighborhood based, this is inescapably a neighborhood-level issue that merits scrutiny to ensure that resources are allocated fairly across schools and that substantial progress is made in narrowing disparities in outcomes. Even in cities with school choice policies that delink school attendance from neighborhood boundaries, the process of improving public schools often requires a school-by-school strategy that addresses the challenges faced by the lowest-performing schools to ensure that all children receive a good education, regardless of where they live or which school they attend.

Chapter 4 approaches education from a people-based perspective, focusing on citywide partnerships to strengthen the overall K–12 education system. Such partnerships can help make the entire education system work better for everyone, fostering economic mobility.

The Houston Independent School District case study illustrates local efforts to improve public schools and address disparities in school quality. Houston has made remarkable progress in improving education outcomes and reducing racial and ethnic disparities by working to ensure that every school provides a high-quality education. Among other strategies to achieve these outcomes, the school district has focused on ensuring that good teachers are hired, making advanced courses available at all

REDUCING DISPARITIES IN EDUCATION OUTCOMES

Houston Independent School District, Houston, Texas

A school district that epitomizes the American melting pot delivers sustained improvements by focusing on teachers as well as students.

HOUSTON HAS AS STRONG A CLAIM AS ANY CITY to being the most diverse in the United States. One in four residents is foreign born, no single ethnic population constitutes a majority, and official welcome signs at the airport are in 60 languages.

Another marker of Houston's extraordinary diversity is the makeup of the student body of the Houston Independent School District (HISD), seventh largest in the country, with a $1.6 billion annual budget, nearly 300 schools, and more than 11,000 teachers. About 100 different languages are spoken by HISD's more than 200,000 students. Thirty percent of students are designated as English-language learners, and 80 percent are eligible for a free or reduced-price school lunch.[33]

For more than a decade, the school district has tested and expanded a wide range of policies and programs aimed at improving opportunities for its students. The results are compelling: in 2013, the federal National Assessment of Educational Progress (NAEP) ranked HISD first or second in the nation in math for students eligible for free and reduced-price lunches, and first or second for African American and Hispanic students.[34] (NAEP is widely considered the most rigorous assessment of the nation's largest school districts in large part because it focuses on actual student learning rather than the ability to take a test.)

HISD is the only two-time winner—in 2002 and 2013—of the Broad Prize for Urban Education, awarded since 2002 to public school systems that have demonstrated the best overall performance and improvement in student achievement while narrowing achievement gaps among low-income students and students of color. The 2013 award noted a 12-percentage-point increase in graduation rates at HISD high schools between 2006 and 2009—double the average increase at the 75 urban districts eligible for the prize.[35]

Equity Strategies, Results, and Challenges

The roots of Houston's school success date to the mid-1990s, when then superintendent Rod Paige, later U.S. secretary of education under President George W. Bush, began testing approaches to adjusting teacher pay according to results in the classroom. These efforts accelerated under the leadership of Abelardo Saavedra, who became superintendent in 2005.

Saavedra took a much bolder, more comprehensive approach to teacher pay, implementing a program that based teacher bonuses on student test scores. "I got stubborn to do it all at once," he recalled later. "I anticipated some controversy, but I didn't think we would get as much pushback as we did. However, when you are completely invested in a movement, odds are that you will survive it."[36]

When Saavedra retired in 2009, 84 Houston schools made the Texas "exemplary" list, up from six in 2005, and HISD ranked as the highest-performing urban school district in the state.[37] Saavedra attributed much of the progress to a focus on teacher performance, which continues to this day. In addition to higher pay for strong performers, the district provides mentors and professional development services to struggling educators and, when necessary, fires those who fall short of HISD standards; more than 900 were let go in a recent two-year period.[38]

Saavedra's successor, Terry Grier, focused intensively on getting more Houston students ready for college and careers. When Grier became superintendent in 2009, only about half of HISD graduates were being accepted into college, and only 15 percent were going on to earn a degree.[39] Grier believed a big reason was that the HISD curriculum was too easy.

"Parents were saying our curriculum wasn't hard enough," Grier later told *U.S. News and World Report*. "Some of the students would say to me, 'Do you think that we're not smart because we're kids of color?' I would probe and ask why, and they'd say, 'Well, we don't have any advanced placement [AP] courses at our schools. We have to go to schools in the affluent neighborhoods to be able to take AP courses.'"[40]

HISD now requires all high schools to offer at least 15 AP courses, and the school district pays for all students to take AP, SAT, and International Baccalaureate exams. "We believe AP classes and exams are for the prepared, not the elite," Grier said.[41] Between 2009 and 2012, the average annual increase in the AP participation rate by Houston's Hispanic students was five times the average for the 75 Broad Prize–eligible districts.

HISD has also pushed the envelope in the area of charter schools. One example is an effort to apply charter practices to turn around 20 of the district's lowest-performing schools—through longer school days and school years, intensive tutoring, and contracted commitments from parents to help their children succeed at school. Early results showed improved student performance in the schools, more so in math than reading.[42]

Richard Carranza, who became the HISD superintendent in 2016, is clear-eyed about the challenges many Houston schools and students still face. In his 2017 State of the Schools address, he pointed to the fact that 60 percent of the district's middle school students read below grade level, and an even higher share of all students are living in poverty and in distressed areas. Carranza called for the same spirit of ambition and optimism that has boosted Houston's school system so far to drive it toward greater progress:

> Some will tell you equity is taking from one school and giving to another or treating all schools the same. Equity is neither. Equity is ensuring that every child at every school and in every community has access to a high-quality education and the resources necessary to be globally competitive.[43]

high schools rather than just those in affluent neighborhoods, and offering charter schools to help improve some of the weakest schools. As is the case in many cities, the Houston school district is independent from the city. But consistent with the broad approach taken throughout this book, the local school district is included within the scope of local actors whose efforts and collaboration are needed to increase economic mobility.

CONCLUSION

The ultimate goal of addressing neighborhood disparities is to ensure that every neighborhood is an *opportunity* neighborhood—providing the amenities and public services that residents need to achieve economic success. This is far simpler to articulate as a goal than to achieve in practice. But as described in this chapter, there are many steps cities can take toward achieving this goal, and a range of examples to draw from as inspiration and guidance.

Increasing the Availability of Affordable Housing in Resource-Rich Areas

In the 1990s, as part of the Moving to Opportunity for Fair Housing demonstration program, HUD offered housing vouchers and assistance in finding housing in low-poverty neighborhoods to families living in public housing located in high-poverty urban areas. The goal was to study the effects on children and adults of moving to areas with low poverty rates. Though the biggest benefits appear to have accrued to the children who moved when they were young—they experienced higher wages and rates of college attendance as young adults[44]—many adults also reported benefits. For example, Lola, a Baltimore resident, told researchers,

> I just got promoted to a higher position. . . . Moving has done wonderful things for me and my family. It has given me an outlook on things that I'm surrounded by. Better neighborhood, better schools for my kids, a better job, great things for me.

Asked what was different about her new neighborhood, Lola replied,

> [It's] totally different. It's a totally different neighborhood be-
> cause there is no drug activity, no kids hanging on the corner,
> no kids fighting each other. . . . It's somewhere you can call
> home. You can just sit down and be comfortable and have no
> worries at all.[45]

Lola's experience illustrates the important influence neighborhood has on child and family well-being, as well as how affordable housing can empower residents to move to areas with less crime, better schools, and better access to jobs. These benefits do not happen by themselves; they require persistent intervention by cities and their partners to create affordable housing opportunities in resource-rich areas and help residents gain access to them.

This section provides an overview of how cities can preserve and expand the availability of affordable housing in resource-rich areas, focusing first on the creation and preservation of dedicated affordable housing, and then on other strategies.

CREATING AND PRESERVING DEDICATED AFFORDABLE HOUSING UNITS

Because housing in resource-rich areas tends to be in high demand, it usually rents or sells at a price well beyond the reach of low- and moderate-income households. For this reason, creating and preserving housing units that are legally restricted to rent or sell at affordable levels is an essential part of ensuring that households of all incomes have access to housing in such areas.

There are literally dozens of local housing policies that communities use to create and preserve dedicated affordable housing in resource-rich areas. Instead of providing an exhaustive review of all these policies, this section presents a series of case studies that illustrate a range of policy options, supplemented with guidance on other promising policies.

To ensure that neighborhoods include housing affordable to people of all incomes, it is important to consider the potential to incorporate such housing into whatever new development is taking place. New development generally occurs in one of three types of neighborhood—new subdivisions, middle- and higher-income neighborhoods, and gentrifying areas. This section first addresses the first two categories together, then the specific case of gentrifying areas, and, finally, resource-rich areas not experiencing new private development.

New Subdivisions and Middle- and Higher-Income Neighborhoods Experiencing New Development

While cities can and should study a range of metrics to develop a nuanced understanding of how opportunity varies from neighborhood to neighborhood, the location of new residential development provides a useful proxy, indicating the market's assessment of where it is desirable to live. It is a reasonably good bet that if people are willing to pay to live in newly developed market-rate housing, that housing is also likely to be attractive to low- and moderate-income households. For this reason, many cities and counties focus on building affordability into new development as a way of expanding access to opportunity for those households. Though there are some subtle differences between the approaches for the two categories of new housing development covered here, in general similar approaches can be applied to encourage creation of affordable housing in new subdivisions and in middle- and higher-income neighborhoods experiencing infill development.

Many tools exist for accomplishing this objective, including density bonuses, reductions in parking requirements, and other incentives that make it financially advantageous for developers to include affordable housing in new development, as well as inclusionary zoning and other mandates that require this outcome. Most landowners and developers prefer that incentives accompany any mandates; otherwise, development feasibility could be imperiled.

Regardless of one's views on the relative merits of incentives versus mandates, it is essential that policies be grounded in a realistic understanding of development costs so that developers can achieve the mandated or incentivized level of affordability. Policies also need to be revised regularly to ensure that they are up-to-date with trends in production costs and achievable rents and sale prices.

The Tysons Corner, Virginia, case study represents a somewhat unusual, but still instructive, example—a classic suburban shopping destination that has chosen to reinvent itself as a transit-oriented community with a large residential population five times its current size. It is included not because many neighborhoods are likely to undergo as dramatic a transformation as Tysons Corner is planning, but because the ambition of the plan required the adoption of a range of aggressive policies for both facilitating new development and ensuring that it includes affordable housing. Other communities can learn much from Tysons's multifaceted and ambitious approach to affordable housing, even if they do not anticipate as much growth as planned at Tysons Corner.

Tysons is unusual in imagining a radically different future for itself. But the policy options it has adopted to build affordability into new development are not unusual and have applicability wherever new development is taking place.

Nearby Montgomery County, Maryland, for example, adopted one of the nation's first inclusionary zoning ordinances, which has generated more than 14,000 affordable housing units since 1976. Unfortunately, many of those affordable units were produced with affordability restrictions that have since expired, reducing the long-term impact of the policy. Learning from this experience, Montgomery County now requires affordable rental units produced through its inclusionary housing policy to remain affordable for 99 years and affordable homeownership units to remain affordable for 30 years. Because the 30-year control period renews every time a home is sold within that period, many of the for-sale units will remain affordable in perpetuity (or near perpetuity).[46]

In April 2016, Fairfax County approved development of the first high-rise condominium in Tysons Corner since the adoption of the transformation plan—the Residences at Arbor Row, a 20-story, 200,000-square-foot ultraluxury trophy condominium building with about 100 units. *Cityline Partners LLC*

INCLUSIVE HOUSING STRATEGY

Tysons Corner, Virginia

A sprawling edge city begins to remake itself as a more walkable, sustainable place, with transit-accessible, mixed-income housing at its core.

FAIRFAX COUNTY, VIRGINIA, home to 1.1 million residents, is the most populous county in the Washington, D.C., region and one of the most prosperous in the nation, with a median household income of nearly $113,000. The county's development since the 1960s and its image today have been shaped by the growth of Tysons Corner, a roughly 1,700-acre area originally marked by the intersection of state Routes 7 and 123. For a half century, "Tysons" has epitomized the commercially successful suburban employment center and retail destination, dominated by large office buildings occupied by white-collar companies and high-end shopping malls.

The enormous economic success of Tysons—it was the nation's 12th-largest central business district as recently as 2014—came over time and at substantial cost in the form of traffic congestion and sprawling development. The number of homes and apartments fell far behind the number of jobs; investment fell short of needs in cultural amenities, green space, and schools; and transit options were limited. The future of Tysons and its role in the region came into question.

That future depends heavily on whether it can reinvent itself as a more complete community. Under the rubric of a "Transforming Tysons" plan, Fairfax County has established goals for 2050: increase the number of Tysons residents to 100,000 (from 19,000), double the number of jobs to 200,000, and ensure that at least three-quarters of the new growth is within a half mile of Metrorail stations. The four Metro stations that opened in Tysons in 2014 are envisioned as a key driver of both real estate value and a more sustainable community.[47]

Fairfax County also intends Tysons to be a mixed-income residential community—a place where construction and service workers, teachers, and others in need of more affordable housing can afford to live. To achieve that goal, it has ambitiously expanded a longstanding county policy that has been a national model for promoting inclusionary housing development.

Equity Strategies, Results, and Challenges

Since 1990, the county has generally required residential development projects, excluding high-rises, to set aside a share of units (usually 5 to 12.5 percent) for households earning 50 to 70 percent of the Washington metropolitan area median income. Landowners receive a density bonus—permission to increase the size of a project—to help mitigate the economic cost of delivering the below-market units.

This affordable dwelling unit (ADU) program had generated more than 2,500 affordable units as of 2016—a roughly equal mix of rental and for-sale housing. Research indicates that Fairfax County ADU homes and apartments are overwhelmingly located in low-poverty neighborhoods and in areas with schools comparable to those in places without ADUs,[48] and that the program has not deterred developers from delivering profitable projects.[49]

By state law, the ADU program does not apply to high-rise buildings—precisely the type of development the county wants near transit under the Tysons transformation plan. Recognizing that this exemption would undermine the opportunity to provide a wider range of housing choice in Tysons, the county created a new complementary policy that could be applied more effectively in the area. Under this new policy, 20 percent of all high-rise units in Tysons must meet affordability requirements, albeit at higher income levels than those in the ADU program. Though low- and mid-rise buildings are still covered by the ADU program, their developers are encouraged to meet the higher percentage standard as well.

As of June 2016, 356 affordable units had been delivered in Tysons under the new policy. Future development up to allowed densities could result in the creation of as many as 4,200 affordable units in the area.[50] Tysons will also generate funding to support affordable housing through payments that office, retail, and hotel development projects must make in return for receiving county approval to build at greater densities—generally either a one-time contribution of $3 per square foot or annual payment of 25 cents per square foot for 16 years. For the development planned as of 2014, this policy (sometimes called a linkage fee) was projected to generate more than $64 million for investment in affordable housing in Tysons through a local housing trust fund.[51]

The capacity of Tysons to become a more equitable community is interlinked with its evolution as a denser, more walkable area and its use of inclusionary development practices and incentives as that evolution occurs. Researcher Christopher Leinberger, whose work has suggested that more-walkable urban places can advance an array of social-equity outcomes as well as deliver superior economic returns, has noted of Tysons: "Many of the neighborhood associations surrounding [Tysons] became supporters of increased density because of the promised walkable urban future. NIMBYs (not in my backyard) became YIMBYs (yes in my backyard)."[52]

Not everyone would agree with the decisions made by Fairfax County in developing Tysons's inclusionary housing policy. For example, in exchange for requiring a higher percentage of inclusionary units, the county raised the income levels of eligible families, reflecting the realities of development feasibility. In order to serve families with very low incomes, the county will need to layer development subsidies through the housing trust fund and other sources onto the inclusionary units.

And while the Tysons policy appears to be working well for rental apartment buildings, it has proved more problematic for for-sale projects. In November 2016, the *Washington Post* reported, "County leaders are considering relaxing the 20 percent expectation for high-rise condominium projects, after developers complained that it will make it harder to secure financing for their typically smaller buildings."[53] The county has worked with the development community to revise the policy to reflect market conditions that have changed since the policy was put in place, and the first condominium project was recently approved.

The Tysons linkage fee provides funding to help ensure there is an adequate supply of affordable housing to support household members who might work, shop, or otherwise interact with area businesses. Among other policy options for generating revenue for affordable housing are interest on government accounts (such as rainy-day funds and unclaimed property funds), interest on real estate escrow accounts, real estate transfer taxes, document recording fees, permit fees, property taxes, tax increment financing, and bond issues. Many communities have identified one or more specific funding sources to finance a housing trust fund that then allocates funding to support affordable housing activities.[54]

Gentrifying Areas

One useful characteristic of inclusionary housing policies like those adopted at Tysons Corner is that they apply wherever development occurs. Thus, they will apply to development that takes place in newly developed communities and middle- and higher-income communities experiencing infill development, as well as in gentrifying areas. Gentrifying areas present a number of special challenges and opportunities, however, that warrant specific discussion.

One important challenge in gentrifying areas is the vulnerability of their low-income residents to displacement. These residents may be unable to afford rapidly rising rents or be at risk of being pushed out by landlords wanting to take advantage of rising values to sell or renovate their buildings. Examples of policies that address this challenge appear later in this chapter.

A second important issue in gentrifying areas—which may constitute both a challenge and an opportunity—is the interaction of timing and risk. Land prices in areas that have not yet gentrified often can be acquired at comparatively low prices, providing an opportunity to develop dedicated affordable housing for low- and moderate-income households as housing prices rise. At the same time, if land prices are low, that generally means the level of risk is high, and the area may never experience a rebound at all or may experience it too slowly to justify the initial investment. In some areas, these risks are great enough to deter desired housing investments, whereas in others they lead to land speculation that drives up land prices in the hope that the neighborhood will gentrify in the future.

Local governments seeking to ensure the long-term availability of affordable housing in gentrifying areas must be mindful of these tradeoffs.

Addressing Gentrification Concerns

GENTRIFICATION IS A CHARGED TERM for which there is no agreed-upon definition. In general, gentrifying areas are characterized by rising rents and home-purchase prices that make it difficult for residents with lower incomes to remain in their homes, as well as by changes in income composition. Many gentrifying areas experience changes in racial and ethnic composition—and some would argue this is a defining characteristic of gentrification. Some studies suggest that displacement from gentrifying areas is not as common as generally understood,[55] but this finding could be a consequence of how gentrification is being measured and defined.

While resolution of these issues is beyond the scope of this book, it should be noted that public policies play a critical role in mitigating concerns associated with gentrification. It is particularly important for cities to have robust policies for protecting residents from displacement and for preserving and expanding the availability of housing in neighborhoods experiencing gentrification pressures.

Cities also need to listen and respond to concerns raised by residents in order to counter the disempowerment often associated with the economic forces jeopardizing residential stability. For example, important cultural issues often accompany gentrification as neighborhoods with strong ethnic associations fear the loss of cultural identity; classic examples include San Francisco's Mission District and New York City's Harlem, associated with Latino and African American culture, respectively. While there are no easy answers to such challenges, cities can help by taking residents' concerns seriously and working in good faith to address and mitigate them.

But the government calculus and role differ somewhat from those of the private sector. For one thing, actions by the local government can affect the timing of neighborhood change and the associated development risks. For example, government investments in public infrastructure—repairing roads and sidewalks, building parks and new schools, etc.—can accelerate the pace of change and decrease the risks associated with development. These investments can be critical for improving the quality of life in neighborhoods and stimulating private development. But it is precisely because of these effects that local governments must have policies in place to promote the inclusion of affordable housing in new development *before* they make these investments.

Cities also should consider implementing policies to acquire land in gentrifying areas for future affordable housing development as early as possible in the cycle of neighborhood change, when land is most affordable. These policies could include, for example:

- **CREATION OF ACQUISITION FUNDS.** These help developers of affordable housing acquire property. Examples include the New York City Acquisition Fund, the Bay Area Transit-Oriented Affordable Housing Fund, and the San Francisco Housing Accelerator Fund. New York City's fund has $210 million available for acquisition and predevelopment financing, capitalized by $8 million in city funding and $32 million from philanthropic foundations. The Bay Area fund has $50 million available to support the development of affordable housing and community facilities near transit, capitalized by a $10 million investment from the Metropolitan Transportation Commission, the transportation planning agency for the nine-county San Francisco Bay area.[56] The newly launched San Francisco Housing Accelerator Fund has about $47 million available, which includes $10 million in city funding, $7 million in philanthropic investment, and $30 million in private capital.

■ **DEDICATION OF PUBLICLY OWNED LAND FOR AFFORDABLE HOUSING.** Many communities have identified opportunities to use land they already own to facilitate the development of affordable housing in targeted neighborhoods. For example, several communities in Massachusetts have adapted school or municipal buildings for affordable housing. Seattle and San Francisco have formal procedures for identifying publicly owned surplus land that could be used for affordable housing.[57] Tax-delinquent properties are another potential source of land for redevelopment, especially if set aside for affordable housing before property values rise to the point where private investors are actively acquiring these properties.

■ **STRATEGIES FOR ACQUIRING AND HOLDING LAND FOR REDEVELOPMENT.** In some cases, land prices may begin to rise well before market demand will support new development. This can occur, for example, near planned transit routes in cities with well-developed transit systems. One solution is for the city to authorize and fund an entity to acquire properties and hold them (often free of property tax) until development is feasible. Denver's Transit-Oriented Development Fund is an example of such an approach. That fund is expected to allow the nonprofit Urban Land Conservancy to purchase sites for the creation and preservation of more than 1,000 units of affordable housing units in current and future transit corridors in and around Denver.[58]

The Sawmill Community Land Trust case study depicts a bottom-up approach to creating and preserving affordable housing in areas at risk of gentrification. Residents of a neighborhood in Albuquerque came together to acquire land where property values were rising and dedicated it to a community land trust. Under this model, the nonprofit trust retains ownership of the property while selling the structures occupying it to homebuyers. With the land appreciation taken largely out of the

Affordable energy-efficient homes in the heart of Old Town Albuquerque, developed by the Sawmill Community Land Trust. *Sawmill Community Land Trust*

Sawmill Community Land Trust, Albuquerque, New Mexico

Neighborhood residents create a development organization that can acquire and redevelop land for affordable uses in an area of escalating property values.

THE ALBUQUERQUE NEIGHBORHOOD known as Sawmill was named for the lumber mills where many of the area's mostly Hispanic residents worked for decades. For most of its history, the community was also "a neighborhood of small houses, mainly adobe, and often owner-built, placed close together on lots that are frequently irregular in shape," according to a 1978 report.[59]

In the early 1980s, residents established a community-based group to organize opposition to a particleboard factory that was polluting the neighborhood. In 2007, when the factory finally closed, the *Albuquerque Journal* noted, "The old particleboard plant, which closed several years ago, had long been a sore spot for those who lived in the area. Some residents for years wanted the plant gone due to environmental concerns, or air pollution and water contamination that was tied to the site."[60]

In the early 1990s, community leaders perceived a new threat: gentrification and potential displacement of longtime lower-income residents. Though the Sawmill neighborhood was still largely industrial and low income in nature, its proximity to downtown, which was starting to see signs of redevelopment, and Old Town Albuquerque, a major tourist destination, made it a prime target for rapid real estate investment.

Property values and rents were increasing without much, if any, benefit to lower-income residents, many of whom worried about being priced out of the community. According to one report, "Between 1981 and 2000, home prices in Sawmill quadrupled, effectively pricing out the low-income residents that historically resided in the area."[61]

Equity Strategies, Results, and Challenges

The Sawmill Action Council, which led the organizing effort against the particleboard plant, sought to create a mechanism that would protect residents from the adverse effects of gentrification while also giving the community a role in redevelopment. Council members learned about the community land trust model, through which nonprofit organizations purchase and retain ownership of land and lease sites to buyers who own their homes. The Sawmill Community Land Trust was founded in 1996 and acted quickly to control a significant parcel—a 27-acre formerly industrial site, the former Duke City Lumber Yard, which it bought from the city.

The trust began to develop a master-planned, mixed-income community called Arbolera de Vida (Orchard of Life). Several years later, it secured an adjacent seven acres—the site of the particleboard factory. As of 2017, the trust has almost fully built out the 34-acre site, with more than 350 homes, including detached single-family for-sale houses, rental apartment properties, and a senior housing community. All the units serve households earning 80 percent or less of the area median income and will remain permanently affordable to the target income group through legal mechanisms set up by the trust.

Following the success of the community land trust, commercial redevelopment has also occurred in the area, including new retail and office space. A five-story luxury hotel was under construction in mid-2017, and industrial properties were being purchased with plans for redevelopment as multistory, mixed-use buildings offering residential units above ground-level commercial space.

Through the trust's acquisition of land and its use of the community land trust model, the households it serves will not be priced out of the housing market as the area continues to transform. Homeowners lease the land from the trust for a nominal, monthly fee through a renewable 99-year ground lease. As a condition of the lease, homeowners agree to resale restrictions on their homes in order to protect their ongoing affordability and to preserve them as affordable housing for future buyers. The rental apartment properties developed by the trust have long-term rent limits as well.

Though the limitations on price appreciation imposed by the land trust model mean that lower-income owners are not able to accumulate the same wealth over time that they otherwise would through home price appreciation, they do enable families to live in a redeveloping area that likely would not be affordable to them otherwise. An account of the history of the Sawmill Community Land Trust suggests that residents were aware of this tradeoff from the outset:

> Though some residents aired concerns about the lack of land ownership in the [community land trust] model, a community elder reminded them that they didn't truly have ownership of their property in any case, either because they were renting or were ill-equipped to control what happened on their land. Former [land trust] executive director Wade Patterson says, "The fact that the work was specifically geared toward controlling housing costs assuaged concerns about gentrification and displacement. The fact that we got a house instead of another factory was something we couldn't argue with."[62]

Ultimately, the ability of the trust to ensure long-term affordability for lower-income residents of Sawmill is limited to the land it controls. Efforts to create broader tools to achieve that goal in the area and other revitalizing parts of Albuquerque, such as inclusionary housing policies, have not been successful to date.

picture, the homes remain affordable over time to one generation of homebuyers after another, even as market rents and home prices rise. Community land trusts and similar approaches—including deed-restricted homeownership and limited-equity cooperatives—are sometimes grouped together under the heading *shared-equity homeownership*

Is It Fair to Limit the Resale Prices of Homes Purchased by Low-Income Households?

APPROACHES TO HOUSING AFFORDABILITY employing shared-equity homeownership, like the community land trust model, preserve long-term affordability through resale restrictions that balance the homebuyer's interest in building wealth with the community's interest in preserving long-term affordability.

Some have questioned whether this is equitable. Whereas market-rate homebuyers have the opportunity to realize the full value of home price appreciation, purchasers of shared-equity homes do not. Whether this is fair is an important question that every shared-equity program wrestles with. The following three observations may help as communities discuss this issue.

■ Without restrictions on resale prices, affordable homeownership programs will fail to maintain long-term affordability in gentrifying areas because the homes will eventually be resold at unaffordable levels. This also has the effect of limiting the number of people who can benefit from public or philanthropic investment.

■ Different resale formulas strike a different balance between the dual goals of individual wealth accumulation and the preservation of long-term affordability. Local programs can set this balance at whatever point they wish.

■ Strong evidence exists that even with resale restrictions, purchasers of shared-equity homes build life-altering wealth through the paydown of the principal balance of their mortgage and their share of home price appreciation.[63]

because they generally use equity-sharing formulas that seek to balance the individual's interest in building wealth through homeownership with the community's interest in ensuring long-term affordability.

Though community land trusts like that at Sawmill are nonprofit organizations, they often receive support from local government in a number of ways, such as through concessionary prices on city-owned land, subsidies to facilitate the acquisition of property, and downpayment assistance for land trust purchasers. Local government representatives also commonly sit on the board of community land trusts, where board representation is shared by nonprofit organizations, local government, and residents.

Even as the Sawmill Community Land Trust demonstrates the success of efforts to provide affordable home purchase opportunities to moderate-income households in a gentrifying area, it illustrates the limitations of focusing only on one policy tool. A community land trust can only ensure the affordability of properties it owns. Complementary policies—such as the other policies discussed in this chapter—are necessary to create and preserve additional affordable housing units in these areas.

Existing Resource-Rich Areas Not Experiencing New Private Development

Incorporating affordable housing into new development is much easier than creating it in places where private development is not generally taking place. But to help low- and moderate-income households gain access to resource-rich areas, cities need to focus on preserving and expanding affordable housing opportunities in existing resource-rich areas, even if they are not experiencing new development.

One initial and essential component of such efforts is to preserve the long-term affordability of any existing dedicated affordable housing developments in these areas. Many of these developments were created decades ago using programs that require affordability to be maintained for a period of time, but then allow owners to leave the affordability program and raise rents to market rates. Given the difficulty of acquiring sites for development in resource-rich areas and obtaining approval and financing for new development, a focus on preserving the affordability of existing affordable housing in these areas is essential.

One critical preservation tool is the Low-Income Housing Tax Credit (LIHTC)—a federal tax credit for the preservation and construction of affordable rental housing, allocated by state (and in some cases local) housing finance agencies. Tax incentives and other incentives also play an important role. In some cases, communities also may need to bring in mission-driven owners to acquire the property. But the first and most important requirement is that cities identify affordable housing properties, determine which are in danger of leaving the subsidized inventory, and prioritize efforts to preserve those properties for the long term.

The LIHTC program can be used to create new affordable rental developments in resource-rich areas as well as to preserve existing affordable developments. While LIHTCs can be used in any location, a number of states have prioritized the use of LIHTC in resource-rich areas. The 2016 Qualified Allocation Plan for the State of Massachusetts, for example, identifies the following as one of its funding priorities for LIHTCs: "Family housing production in neighborhoods and communities that provide access to opportunities, including, but not limited to, jobs, transportation, education, and public amenities."

Though the rules governing the award of LIHTCs are generally made at the state level, localities can influence the location of units developed through these credits. They can do this by prioritizing projects in resource-rich areas for locally controlled funds (such as funds provided through the HOME Investment Partnership program) that are often necessary as "gap funding" to cover the difference between project costs and the funding available through the syndication of LIHTC credits and supportable debt. For example, in its 2016 request for proposals for the HOME program,[64] Harris County, Texas, identified highly resource-rich areas as one of several funding priorities for its limited resources. This likely will have the effect not only of directing the use of the county's HOME funds, but also of leveraging LIHTC projects that require HOME funds to serve as gap funding to make projects work financially. Cities can also create incentives for developers to use other city-administered subsidy programs in such areas, including programs funded through housing trust funds and housing bond issues, among other sources.

Another step cities can take is to acquire individual units, houses, or small developments in resource-rich neighborhoods and assemble them into a scattered-site portfolio. The King County, Washington, Housing Authority (KCHA) case study (see page 83) provides an example of this approach. KCHA, which serves a large urban area adjacent to Seattle, has acquired a portfolio of Class B apartments that it rents at levels affordable for moderate-income households, prioritizing units in resource-rich areas for acquisition. KCHA also has taken steps to make units in resource-rich areas affordable to extremely low-income households by project-basing Housing Choice Vouchers in these units—providing a deep subsidy for affordable housing by repurposing federal resources and therefore requiring little or no municipal funding.

OTHER STRATEGIES FOR HELPING HOUSEHOLDS GAIN ACCESS TO AND AFFORD RESOURCE-RICH AREAS

Though the creation and preservation of dedicated affordable housing units is an essential component of efforts to preserve and expand affordable housing in resource-rich areas, it is not sufficient on its own. A brief review follows of key complementary policies in the other three major domains of the National Community of Practice on Local Housing Policy's emerging housing policy framework:

- promoting affordability by increasing the overall supply of housing and lowering barriers and costs to development and production;

- helping renters and homebuyers gain access to and afford units in the private market; and

- ensuring housing stability and quality.

Promoting Affordability by Increasing the Overall Supply of Housing and Lowering Barriers and Costs

Efforts in the first of the complementary areas tackle the main challenges causing rents and home prices to rise faster than incomes in many urban areas—regulatory barriers such as unnecessarily restrictive limitations on housing density and unpredictable and lengthy entitlement processes. These and similar barriers increase the cost of development and make it difficult for the private market to respond to increases in the demand for housing with increased supply.[65] These supply constraints lead rents and home prices to rise faster than they would with a more elastic supply and also lead developers to focus limited development opportunities on the high end of the market, where they can best recoup their costs, rather than on a broader spectrum of housing needs.

Though efforts to reduce these regulatory barriers will not in and of themselves allow low- and moderate-income households to afford housing in resource-rich areas, they have an important complementary role to play in association with the tools described earlier. Developers seeking to build dedicated affordable housing in resource-rich areas face many of the same barriers as developers of market-rate housing. These barriers increase the costs of that development, leading to an increase in subsidy needs or, in some cases, a determination that a proposed affordable project is not feasible. Reduction of barriers helps make development of dedicated affordable housing units more feasible.

Such barriers may also increase opportunities for opponents of new development to stop an affordable housing development in its tracks. For example, when the densities needed to make development viable are available only through a zoning variance or special use permit, neighborhood residents opposed to affordable housing will have an opportunity to stop the development. This opportunity for derailment would not have been available had viable densities been offered to owners as of right.

Efforts to reduce barriers can also play a more indirect role in facilitating affordability. Because housing markets are regional in nature, an overall shortage of supply can lead to rent and home price inflation that affects a large share of the region, including resource-rich and gentrifying areas. A more elastic regional housing supply helps reduce these price pressures, making rents and home prices more affordable to existing and new residents, as well as land acquisition more feasible for the development of affordable homes.

To reduce barriers to new development, cities should examine their zoning processes to ensure that they are as predictable as possible and provide viable development opportunities as of right rather than through more discretionary processes. This is not to say that cities should give up control over the development process. Cities can and should determine the appropriate level of density in each neighborhood and the associated incentives or requirements for affordable housing. But once they make these determinations, it is in their interests and the interests of the community to allow that development to take place without discretionary processes that introduce delay and increase risk—both of which lead to higher development costs often passed on to consumers as higher rents or home prices.

Because time is money in the development business, cities should also examine how to speed up their permitting processes. Some cities have adopted expedited processes, either for all development or for affordable housing development specifically. These expedited procedures can cut months or even years off the development process, lowering the costs of both dedicated affordable and market-rate development.

While most housing in resource-rich areas that rents or sells at market rates will be outside the reach of low- and moderate-income households, certain development types may be more affordable. Accessory dwelling units, for example, are particularly well suited to creating housing options that are unsubsidized yet affordable. Sometimes called granny flats, accessory dwelling units are units added to a single-family home that often rent for less than the prevailing rents or home prices due to their small size. Zoning rules often bar such units, so one easy step is for cities to revise those rules to allow them. Cities can also encourage their development by educating the public about this development option and by making subsidies or below market-rate financing available for homeowners interested in developing such units (perhaps conditioned on agreements to cap rents).

Accessory dwelling units are receiving increased attention in high-cost areas as a source of new housing. California, for example, passed a law in 2016 making it easier for homeowners to construct them.[66] In New York City, the BASE (Basement Apartments Safe for Everyone) pilot program is examining whether and to what extent existing basements could be brought up to code and recognized as part of the city's housing supply. This should help expand the supply of legal apartments available for rent.

Helping Renters and Homebuyers Gain Access to and Afford Units in the Private Market

With more than 2 million in use nationwide, Housing Choice Vouchers are a critically important component of the affordable housing infrastructure. Though studies confirm that families using vouchers are less likely to live in high-poverty areas than are residents of public housing or older project-based Section 8 developments,[67] these families are also fairly unlikely to end up in resource-rich areas unless special efforts are made by public housing agencies or their partners. For this reason—and because three-fourths of the households with newly issued federal Housing Choice Vouchers must have an extremely low income—helping voucher holders use their vouchers to rent housing in resource-rich areas is one important way to assist low-income households in affording housing in such areas.

These efforts have several important components:

- **ADJUSTING PAYMENT STANDARDS TO LEVELS SUFFICIENT FOR RESIDENTS TO AFFORD UNITS IN RESOURCE-RICH AREAS.** Under federal law, local public housing agencies have the discretion to adjust the payment standards that determine the maximum subsidy available through a voucher (which in turn determines the maximum rents participating households can afford through the subsidy). An agency may select a single payment standard for its entire service area or vary the standard by neighborhood. Agencies interested in helping voucher holders obtain housing in resource-rich areas should ensure that payment standards in those areas are set at levels sufficient to enable voucher holders to gain access to rental housing there.

- **PROVIDING MOBILITY COUNSELING.** Most households participating in the Housing Choice Voucher Program will be more familiar with certain neighborhoods than others. Even if payment standards are set at levels sufficient to enable a voucher holder to rent in a resource-rich area, the household may not look in those areas because they are unfamiliar with them. Mobility counseling helps interested voucher holders become aware of rental opportunities in such areas. Depending on the local counseling program, it may also help voucher holders visit a property and interview for a unit, as well as recruit owners of housing in resource-rich areas to participate in the program.

- **PROVIDING ASSISTANCE WITH SECURITY DEPOSITS AND FIRST AND LAST MONTH'S RENT.** While the Housing Choice Voucher Program provides a substantial subsidy to enable participating households to afford their monthly rent, it does not provide funding for a security deposit or the first or last month's rent. Owners in resource-rich areas are likely to require a higher security deposit than owners of housing in other areas (because the rents are higher) and may be more likely to ask the resident to provide first and last month's rent upon signing the lease. By providing voucher holders with assistance in meeting those costs, localities can help facilitate moves to resource-rich areas and provide an incentive for households to consider them. A household that might be on the fence about relocating might also benefit from help with moving costs.

The King County Housing Authority case study describes how that agency has used many of these tools to help voucher holders gain access to resource-rich areas, including by changing the payment standard and providing mobility counseling, as well as by acquiring units in scattered sites and using its project-based vouchers for specific units.

As a Moving to Work agency, KCHA has special authority to vary HUD's program rules. While KCHA has used this flexibility well to expand the availability of affordable housing in resource-rich areas, all public housing agencies—regardless of Moving to Work status—can take advantage of many of the same tools. For example, all housing agencies have the right to raise voucher payment standards to 110 percent of the fair market rent and to adopt small-area fair market rents in which those rents are set at the zip code level, allowing voucher holders to afford higher rents in higher-cost areas. Similarly, all housing agencies have the right to project-base up to 20 percent of their Housing Choice Vouchers in particular developments. In addition, under recently passed legislation,[68] public housing agencies can project-base up to an additional 10 percent of vouchers to help veterans or people experiencing homelessness, to provide supportive housing to seniors or people with disabilities, or to help those in areas where the poverty rate is 20 percent or less. Because resource-rich areas will almost always meet the last criterion, the cap is essentially 30 percent of vouchers that could be used to secure affordable units in such areas through project-basing.

Another important strategy for helping voucher holders gain access to resource-rich areas is to adopt a local ordinance prohibiting private

A Boys & Girls Club center delivers out-of-school-time programming at the King County Housing Authority's Eastside Terrace public housing property in Bellevue. *King County Housing Authority, William Wright Photography*

ACCESS TO OPPORTUNITY NEIGHBORHOODS

King County Housing Authority, King County, Washington

A county housing agency, working with private developers and apartment operators, works to help very low-income families gain access to housing in resource-rich communities.

THE KING COUNTY HOUSING AUTHORITY (KCHA) provides rental housing and rental assistance to more than 48,000 people, about 40 percent of whom are children. About half the authority's residents live in the 115 apartment properties it either owns or controls, and half rent housing in the private market with the help of federal housing vouchers the authority administers. Many of the households served by KCHA are very poor, with annual average incomes below $20,000.[69]

KCHA serves King County—consisting mainly of suburban communities and very small cities and towns—except for Seattle and Renton (population 91,000), each of which has its own housing authority. KCHA's area presents a challenging geographical and jurisdictional environment in which to operate. King County is one of the largest counties in the United States—more than 2,100 square miles, about the size of Delaware—and is home to more than

2 million people, about 600,000 of whom live in Seattle. King County has experienced substantial population growth in recent years and expects to add 300,000 people by 2031, many attracted by the area's thriving technology sector and natural beauty.[70]

However, King County's prosperity is not evenly distributed, and income inequality is increasing. The county's current comprehensive plan expresses concern about "two King Countys depending on where people live, and such lack of equity throughout our region puts us at a disadvantage to grow our economy for the benefit of all of our residents, unless we take affirmative action and begin to close the gap on such inequities."[71]

This challenge plays out in stark geographic terms. In general, the southern part of the county, including areas adjacent to Seattle, is characterized by lower incomes and poorer-performing schools compared with communities in eastern King County, which include affluent suburbs such as Bellevue, Kirkland, and Redmond. In a region in which opportunity is tied tightly to location, the availability of affordable housing in the right locations can make it possible for more people to benefit from high-performing schools and other key amenities.

Equity Strategies, Results, and Challenges

To address these challenges, KCHA is executing a multiyear plan to expand the availability of housing in resource-rich areas affordable to some of the region's lowest-income residents. Since 2003, KCHA has been one of 39 national Moving to Work housing authorities. The designation, by the U.S. Department of Housing and Urban Development, enables the agency to op-erate under more flexible federal rules than otherwise would apply. KCHA has employed this flexibility in innovative ways to enable more of the households it serves to live in more resource-rich areas with high-performing schools.

To expand access to resource-rich areas (which KCHA calls "opportunity areas"), KCHA has creatively used its regulatory flexibility to increase the level of rent that its housing vouchers can cover for very low-income house-holds. In 2003, KCHA split its service area into two zones, raising the voucher payment standards in the zone with higher rents to make it easier for voucher holders to obtain housing there. In 2016, it fine-tuned its approach, splitting its service area into five zones, which allowed it to more closely tie voucher payment standards to local rent variations. As a result of these changes, more than one in five of the authority's tenant-based vouchers are being used to rent housing in "high-opportunity" or "very high-opportunity neighborhoods," according to a methodology developed by the Ohio State University Kirwan Institute for the Study of Race and Ethnicity.

KCHA also has experimented with a pilot program to help low-income families find housing in resource-rich areas more easily and better navigate the local school system. Between 2013 and 2017, KCHA operated the Community Choice Program, which provided housing counseling and search assistance, financial assistance, and post-move counseling. Though it produced promising outcomes—about 60 percent of counseled families who moved chose to move to an opportunity area—the pilot program was small and relatively expensive, raising questions about the ability to take it to scale. Building on its experience with that program, KCHA has joined with other public housing authorities to work with a team of researchers led by Raj Chetty to rigorously evaluate a range of mobility strategies to determine how to efficiently and effectively support moves to resource-rich areas.

KCHA has also targeted some of its rental-housing development funding to apartment properties in strong neighborhoods. By attaching (known as "project-basing") vouchers to existing structures in this manner, the authority provides an incentive to developers and landlords in those areas to make apartments available to very low-income families without increasing their cost. The agency also uses these vouchers in properties it purchases from private owners, which otherwise might be converted to higher-rent properties. To date, over 40 percent of the 2,000 vouchers the agency has project-based have been in neighborhoods defined as "high opportunity" or "very high opportunity" according to the Kirwan Institute criteria.

KCHA is an innovator in part because it does not view its mission as a housing agency solely in terms of units built and managed. The agency's ultimate priority is its residents, especially children. The agency's 2017 annual plan states: "Close to 14,000 children are living in KCHA's federally subsidized housing at any given time. Their academic success is the cornerstone of our efforts to prevent multi-generational cycles of poverty and promote economic mobility. KCHA continues to make successful education outcomes an integral element of our core mission by actively partnering with local education stakeholders around shared outcomes."[72]

In addition to its housing voucher initiatives to help families gain access to housing in strong school districts, the agency has built 15 youth centers and three Head Start facilities; created partnerships with three school districts where significant numbers of KCHA's resident students live; and worked with local community-based providers to deliver out-of-school-time educational programming supported by nationally emerging research on best practices. The agency has also created an innovative program to provide "rapid rehousing" of homeless families with children.

KCHA is constantly looking for new ways to leverage its impact by partnering with area businesses and nonprofits and local governments. Whenever the economics make sense for the agency, it acquires existing affordable properties in stronger neighborhoods that it maintains as low-cost housing for moderate-income households; some of these properties have restricted rents through the Low-Income Housing Tax Credit program or other subsidy programs, while others are unsubsidized.

In 2016, KCHA invested $2 million in a new regional revolving loan fund that provides low-cost financing to developers for the acquisition of property in transit-accessible areas to preserve and create affordable homes for low- and moderate-income households. The Regional Equitable Development Initiative (REDI) Fund requires that each existing or new property have a share of affordable units available for those making 80 percent or less of the area median income. In addition, properties must be within a half mile of a rail station or a quarter mile of a bus stop.[73]

owners from refusing to participate in the Housing Choice Voucher Program. Though owners remain free to reject applicants they think will not make good tenants, such policies help reduce the discrimination experienced by voucher holders who otherwise could afford to live in a particular unit in a resource-rich area with their voucher. More broadly, stronger enforcement of the Fair Housing Act's protections against discrimination on the basis of race, national origin, disability, or family status—as well as education to expand awareness of these protections—is important for helping maximize opportunities for voucher holders and other low- and moderate-income households.

Some communities also offer assistance to help low- or moderate-income households become homeowners, such as assistance with closing costs or downpayments. Generally, when this assistance is at a fairly low level, it is structured as a grant.

As the per-household level of homeownership subsidies increases, communities often become more interested in preserving the subsidy as a community asset, which may lead initially to loans and perhaps eventually to a shared-equity homeownership approach like the Sawmill Community Land Trust. While circumstances will vary from community to community, in general the high costs of for-sale homes in resource-rich areas will mean that the level of per-household subsidy needed to enable a low- or moderate-income homebuyer to afford to live there will be high. This suggests that, to obtain access to housing in resource-rich areas, targeted homebuyers will need deeper subsidies provided through shared-equity homeownership rather than shallow subsidies provided through grants for closing costs.

Ensuring Housing Stability and Quality

If affordable housing is thought of only in terms of bricks and mortar, the responsibility ends with the creation or preservation of an affordable unit. But to really provide low- and moderate-income households with meaningful access to resource-rich areas, those households need to have not only access to those communities, but also assurance that they can stay in them. This requires additional policies designed to help renters and homeowners maintain housing stability.

This issue is particularly important in gentrifying communities, where rising property values and rents may put significant pressure on existing low- and moderate-income residents, leading to instability or displacement.

For example, low- and moderate-income homeowners in gentrifying areas may experience rising property taxes that make it difficult for them to afford to stay in their neighborhood even as it becomes a more attractive place to live. To address this problem, some communities have adopted property tax circuit breakers that limit property tax increases for low- and moderate-income households. To address the risk of displacement due to the physical deterioration of older homes, some communities have developed programs that offer funding for home repair to elderly and other low-income residents, either as grants or as silent second mortgages that do not need to be repaid until the home is sold.

Rising rents also pose a challenge for low- and moderate-income renters in gentrifying areas. While communities are unlikely to be able to stop a long-term rise in rents for unrestricted properties, they can put in place policies that reduce the impact of these increases on area residents, providing them with a greater opportunity to control whether and under what circumstances they relocate. Rent stabilization policies, for example, often allow rents to float to market levels between tenancies, but then limit annual increases so residents who can afford the initial rent are not forced to move due to rapid rent increases. Some communities have also revised their landlord-tenant law to limit evictions to cases of "good cause," such as nonpayment of rent or criminal activity. These policies protect residents in good standing from being evicted by owners seeking to reposition the property. In some cases, free or low-cost legal representation may also be needed to help residents take advantage of these protections.

Though residents of dedicated affordable housing units in resource-rich areas do not face the possibility of rapidly rising rents, they remain vulnerable to displacement if they experience a short-term job loss or health crisis that makes it difficult to pay the rent. Deep rental-subsidy programs such as project-based Section 8 adjust the rents in the event of declining income, but other programs such as LIHTC do not. Cities can help promote housing stability in these cases through programs that in an emergency provide back rent to a resident in need.

Residents of dedicated affordable housing in resource-rich areas may face other issues that affect their ability to maintain housing stability. Depending on the area, residents may need adjustments to public transportation schedules and fares to ensure that they can get to work affordably within a reasonable commuting time, or need counseling to help them establish support networks (e.g., child care and access to medical care) to replace the ones they may have left behind in their previous neighborhood.

CONCLUSION

By taking a comprehensive approach that uses policy tools from four broad categories, cities can help increase opportunities for low- and moderate-income households to gain access to, afford, and remain in resource-rich areas. Though it is important for cities to combine complementary policies to increase their impact, they do not need to adopt every possible policy in order to make progress. Rather than seek to implement the largest number of policies, cities should be strategic and strive to select and adapt a range of policies that enable them to make meaningful progress in increasing the availability of affordable housing in resource-rich areas.

CHAPTER 4

People-Based Strategies

AS DISCUSSED IN CHAPTER 2, many systems contribute to an individual's ability to advance economically. This book so far has focused on place-based strategies—including community development and affordable housing strategies—because of the critical role place plays in ensuring access to the services, resources, and systems that individuals need to thrive. This chapter explores four additional building blocks critical to an individual's ability to achieve economic mobility:

- comprehensive public education, including

  - early childhood education,

  - elementary and secondary education, and

  - support for college studies and completion;

- financial health;

- workforce and skills development; and

- small business development.

These are termed *people-based* strategies to distinguish them from the place-based approaches covered in chapter 3.

These four systems focus on ensuring that individuals have the tools, skills, and institutions needed to take make economic progress. Even as cities work to improve the places where people live, they must also strengthen the systems through which people obtain an education, find jobs with a career path, start and scale up small businesses, and secure their financial future.

As emphasized in chapter 2, providing these systems should not be seen as an afterthought. Cities can earn a strong return on investment from these activities in the form of higher wages, lower crime, less financial disruption, and stronger business communities. Despite these benefits, many cities continue to think of these areas as "individual services," often heavily reliant on grant funding with patchy availability throughout the city. This chapter challenges cities to think about these four areas at the systems level and consider how improvements in these systems might strengthen the city economically even as it becomes more equitable.

Some of these supports, such as elementary and secondary education and efforts to build financial health, are needed for the simple reason that they teach skills everyone needs. Other supports are needed to help individuals overcome barriers they may encounter as they seek to advance economically, such as financial challenges that make it difficult to complete college, a skills deficit that makes it hard to get higher-paying work, or lack of capital to start a small business.

All people need some form of support at some point in their lives. While some individuals are fortunate enough to be born into families that can provide these supports privately, others are in families unable to provide these supports or are on their own. By helping individuals acquire necessary skills and overcome barriers to advancement, cities can address the inequities that arise from disparities in family resources and increase the likelihood of economic success for both individuals and the city as a whole.

Comprehensive Public Education

A full review of the public education system and how it might be improved is well beyond the scope of this book. But given the fundamental importance of education in shaping children's life outcomes, it is important to underscore the need for cities to focus on improving education. Chapter 3 took a place-based approach to discuss the efforts of Houston's public school system to reduce disparities in school quality so children can get a good education regardless of where they live. This chapter takes a people-based approach focused on opportunities for improving the quality of education throughout a school system to boost outcomes for everyone.

The StrivePartnership case study, from the region spanning Cincinnati and northern Kentucky, centers on the partnership's role in coordinating the activities of more than 300 partners to produce measurable improvements in children's education outcomes. The partnership is notable both for the substance of its education strategy and for its application of a "collective impact" approach that communities could apply in other contexts. Among other lessons from the case study are the following:

- With hundreds of organizations working on different approaches to improving children's education, a critical need exists for a coordinating body that can facilitate communication among the organizations, identify opportunities for partnerships and reduced duplication of services, and identify gaps in the web of support.

- The education needs of individuals are vast, starting with effective parental engagement for infants and toddlers and progressing to preschool, elementary school, high school, and college or other postsecondary education. As the partners in StrivePartnership determined, these pieces are linked: education deficits early in life can lead to accumulated disadvantages that inhibit success later. Therefore, StrivePartnership focuses on the full range of an individual's education needs, from cradle to career.

- Though resources are required in order to carry out the tasks well, the collection, reporting, and analysis of outcomes data can help focus a community on a problem that needs to be addressed, as well as identify whether progress is being made and whether adjustments are needed to improve outcomes.

- The transparency created by a more coordinated education system can help local funders better identify opportunities to contribute to a stronger system.

StrivePartnership, Cincinnati and Northern Kentucky

Educators, business leaders, elected officials, and local foundations align efforts to create a data-driven, "cradle-to-career" system to improve the prospects for low-income children.

THE 2001 SHOOTING of an unarmed African American youth in Cincinnati's Over-the-Rhine neighborhood ignited several days of unrest that included hundreds of injuries and arrests and damage to 140 businesses. Addressing the fallout and its underlying causes became a civic priority for the next several years. Much of the leadership came from a group of 15 corporations and foundations called Better Together Cincinnati.

The collaboration would prove enduring and lay the groundwork for an even more comprehensive, far-reaching effort to help a growing number of students in Cincinnati and northern Kentucky leave high school better prepared for college. With Ohio and Kentucky ranking near the bottom in college-degree attainment by their young people, in the mid-2000s teachers and school superintendents, as well as area employers, agreed that major change was needed.

The situation was vexing because a number of organizations were, in fact, working to improve education outcomes in the region. In the words of one analyst, these organizations "were working hard to build a better future for the area's youth, but were often providing siloed services and using distinctly different approaches. Not surprisingly, the result was a community and education system that was 'program rich' but 'system poor,' according to Dr. O'dell Owens, president of Cincinnati State Technical and Community College."[1] A new way of thinking—and a new system for acting—was needed. That new approach was StrivePartnership.

Equity Strategies, Results, and Challenges

StrivePartnership's founders included Nancy Zimpher, then president of the University of Cincinnati; Michael Graham, president of Xavier University; James Votruba, president of Northern Kentucky University; and the superintendents of the school districts of Covington and Newport, Kentucky, and Cincinnati. Over time, the partnership enlisted more than 300 partner organizations, ranging from executives with the largest local employers and chari-ties to small, community-based organizations and schools.

Though StrivePartnership's leaders convened initially to focus on college preparedness, they quickly realized that only a more holistic view of the chal-lenges facing low-income students—examining the continuum of the educa-tion experience—would yield systemic change.

Recalled Robert Reifsnyder, president of the United Way of Greater Cincin-nati, "Someone said, 'We're focusing on the ninth grade, but these problems really start in middle school.' Someone else said, 'Truth be told, it starts in grade school.' Someone else said, 'Listen folks, if we don't get started by kin-dergarten, the battle's half over.' And finally we said, 'This is a preschool issue: it's about kindergarten readiness.'"[2]

The breakthrough insight of StrivePartnership was that measurable success and progress would not be driven by yet another new program, but rather by all the existing efforts adopting a common set of goals and metrics. Another key ingredient was to identify consensus indicators in the major areas along the education continuum—kindergarten readiness, early-grade reading, middle-grade math, high school graduation, postsecondary enrollment, and postsec-ondary degree completion. The third leg of the stool was a commitment to rigorous data collection and evidence-based decision making, with regular reporting to the public.

The partnership started to gain widespread attention as it reported its results. In 2011, StrivePartnership's five-year results included improvements in 40 of the 53 education outcomes it measured, including a 9 percent increase in kindergarten readiness, an 11 percent increase in high school graduations, and a 10 percent increase in college enrollment.[3] More recent data show that 91 percent of the partnership's indicators for student outcomes are improving in Cincinnati and northern Kentucky. For example, kindergarten readiness is up 14 percentage points to 58 percent and third-grade reading achievement for Cin-cinnati Public Schools students is up 18 percentage points since the baseline year to 73 percent.

The partnership's priorities have consistently evolved and expanded in re-sponse to evidence and the involvement of additional partners. Over the past several years, the partnership has directed significant resources to improving early literacy. Three notable initiatives are:

→

■ **THE CINCINNATI PRESCHOOL PROMISE.** A community organizing and advocacy strategy to expand access to two years of high-quality preschool, the Cincinnati Preschool Promise led to approval of a 2016 ballot measure securing $15 million of new Cincinnati Public Schools funding each year for five years for preschool expansion.

■ **EVERY CHILD CAPITAL VENTURE PHILANTHROPY FUND.** The fund invests philanthropic resources in early literacy interventions that have both a business case justifying public funding and a public sector partner secured at the outset to take over the investment long term.

■ **IMPACTU AND THE THIRD GRADE READING NETWORK.** These programs, being led in partnership with Cincinnati Children's Hospital Medical Center, are focused on building continuous improvement capability in systems change leaders. Cincinnati Children's Hospital, a nationally recognized leader in quality improvement, has recently adopted third-grade reading skills as a measure of child health and well-being.

By 2010, national interest in StrivePartnership's collective-impact approach was growing. StrivePartnership founding director Jeff Edmondson took the opportunity to expand the work, launching a national network in partnership with Living Cities and the Coalition of Urban Serving Universities. The net-

While StrivePartnership focuses on improving education outcomes, its approach to identifying a core community need and bringing parties together to coordinate approaches, agree on outcomes, and collect and analyze data to track progress is applicable to many other social problems as well. Known as "collective impact," the approach requires a coordinating entity—sometimes called a quarterback—to serve as the convener and tracker of outcome data.

Financial Health

The financial health of a city and that of its residents are clearly intertwined. According to the Urban Institute, financial insecurity manifests itself in unpaid taxes, unpaid utility bills, and evictions, which directly affect a city's bottom line.[4] The costs range widely from city to city—from

work, now known as StriveTogether, began with five communities, providing expertise and strategic assistance to cradle-to-career partnerships across the country. It now includes 70 community partnerships in 33 states and the District of Columbia, and has engaged more than 10,000 local organizations, affecting more than 8 million students.[5]

To ensure that the work remains rigorous and of high quality, StriveTogether has developed the Theory of Action, a continuum of benchmarks for building and sustaining civic infrastructure, which it uses to measure a community's progress. Communities that see 60 percent of indicators in six cradle-to-career outcome areas maintained or improved are labeled Proof Points. In 2016, the StrivePartnership was designated the network's first Proof Point community. StriveTogether's goal is to have five Proof Point communities in the network by 2018.

StrivePartnership has learned that implementation of its model is not easy. Establishing trust and a common understanding among educators and business leaders can be challenging, StrivePartnership partners say. Funding matters, too: every local cradle-to-career initiative needs staff and organizational infrastructure, and, of course, schools themselves need adequate resources to meet the basic needs of their students.

$8 million to $18 million in New Orleans to $280 million to $646 million in New York City. Moreover, individual financial health is a critical foundation for the rest of a city's economic-mobility agenda. Without the products and services that help them manage uncertainty and transform income into assets, even people who are employed full time or run successful small businesses can become financially insecure.

CITY SYSTEMS THAT PROMOTE FINANCIAL SECURITY

Cities are well positioned to create systems that promote the financial health of their residents, using their power to convene a wide variety of partners, test new models, connect with vulnerable residents, and leverage their infrastructure to achieve scale. In fact, the most promising models for advancing financial health involve integrating services into workforce, housing, and small-business service-delivery systems described throughout this book.

This is not a new role for cities. In the early 2000s, research from the Brookings Institution showed the value of the earned-income tax credit (EITC) to U.S. cities, with one report asserting that the EITC resulted in greater investment in urban areas than all other federal programs, and that the failure of millions of low-income residents to claim the EITC was resulting in the loss of billions of dollars of income.[6] Many cities, including Philadelphia, Miami, Baltimore, and Chicago, began organizing citywide campaigns to connect residents with free tax-preparation services.

When San Francisco realized that an important asset-building opportunity was being lost because individuals did not have bank accounts, it launched Bank On to bring banks and nonprofits together to encourage low-income people to open their first bank account, leading hundreds of cities to follow its example. In New York City, then mayor Michael Bloomberg recognized that the city's service-delivery infrastructure provided a unique platform from which to connect financially marginalized people with financial coaches. He established the city's first Office of Financial Empowerment (OFE) as a critical part of his poverty-alleviation agenda.

In 2012, San Francisco, New York City, and 13 other cities came together to launch a new nonprofit, the Cities for Financial Empowerment Fund, dedicated to testing and scaling up the most promising municipality-led financial empowerment models. Nearly two decades of efforts to increase EITC filings, encourage residents to open bank accounts, and boost awareness of harmful financial products taught these cities that information alone will not change an individual's financial behavior or decisions. To truly change the trajectory of their financial health and advance equity among a city's most economically vulnerable residents, individuals need real-time, actionable advice and financial products designed to meet their needs.[7]

FOCUSING ON FINANCIAL HEALTH

The financial education field has evolved considerably over the past decade, thanks to program evaluations, new insights from the fields of behavioral science and design thinking, and advances in technology. Today, experts recommend programs and activities that help individuals achieve a state of *financial health* or *financial well-being*—terms used interchangeably. The Consumer Financial Protection Bureau (CFPB) defines financial well-being as a state in which households

- have control over day-to-day, month-to-month finances;
- have the capacity to absorb a financial shock;
- are on track to meet their financial goals; and
- have the financial freedom to make the choices that allow them to enjoy life.[8]

Rather than focus on a static measure such as income, net worth, or post-training knowledge, this definition is flexible, accommodating different life goals, values, and changing circumstances.

With this definition in mind, several leading organizations have put forth tools that allow service providers to measure their clients' progress toward financial health and calibrate their programs to meet their clients where they are financially. Among the leading resources are the following:

- "Eight Ways to Measure Financial Health," from the Center for Financial Services Innovation;
- A toolkit for financial educators to measure financial well-being, from the CFPB: www.consumerfinance.gov/financial-well-being;
- "Financial Coaching: An Asset Building Strategy," from the University of Wisconsin–Madison's Center for Financial Security;

Programs and Services That Build Financial Capability

The following are some of the practices cities and their partners have used to help people build financial capability. While this list can serve as a helpful starting point, cities should review the latest research on successful approaches and analyze needs and existing resources to ensure that they are developing an effective strategy.

■ Financial education integrated into the K–12 curriculum.

■ Financial coaching to help individuals improve their credit, pay down high-interest debt, more effectively use mainstream financial services, build savings, and develop and apply household budgets.

■ Homeownership education and counseling to help people determine whether they want to and are ready to pursue homeownership and, if so, help them prepare for and sustain ownership.

■ Asset-building vehicles—such as children's savings accounts, individual development accounts, and the U.S. Department of Housing and Urban Development's Family Self-Sufficiency Program—that help people build assets they can use to weather crises and meet their long-term financial needs.

■ Retirement savings programs and counseling to help people prepare for a financially secure retirement.

■ Free tax preparation and earned-income tax credit outreach to help people avoid tax-filing fees and unnecessary refund-anticipation loans, and learn about the tax benefits to which they may be entitled.

■ Services for those without bank accounts, including outreach to educate them about the importance of having an account and how to open one, as well as innovative financial products that help expand the number of people who have accounts.

■ Bankruptcy, eviction, and foreclosure counseling to help residents in financial distress get access to assistance and develop an approach for regaining their financial health.

- "Enabling Financial Capability along the Road to Financial Inclusion," from the Center for Financial Inclusion at Accion; and

- "Financial Coaching to Improve Financial Well-Being," from the CFPB.

Cities should use these tools and others available to determine the most pressing needs in their community and design the financial empowerment system to be responsive. For example, a study by the Urban Institute showed that in Detroit, two-thirds of residents have a subprime credit score or no credit score, and that 68 percent of residents have delinquent debt.[9] This indicated that for many Detroit residents, managing debt and improving credit are crucial first steps for ensuring stable housing or starting a business. Consequently, Detroit plans to implement financial coaching programs to help residents reduce debt and improve credit, which will help them purchase a home or stay in a home where they already live.

Even modest improvements in financial health can have a major payoff for residents and cities. Research shows that $2,000 in liquid savings can help families weather life events such as a temporary job loss, a decrease in hourly earnings, or a big medical expense or other unexpected financial burden. Researchers at the Pew Charitable Trust found that 71 percent of children born to parents in the bottom quartile of income, but who are regular savers, move to a higher quartile in income as adults, compared with 50 percent of children whose parents did not save regularly.[10] Children with even a small savings account are seven times more likely to attend college than those without an account.[11]

The case study reviews the activities of the New York City OFE, which oversees a network of more than 30 financial empowerment centers throughout the city, helping residents pay down debt, build savings, and take advantage of the EITC and other tax credits. The OFE emphasizes

Office of Financial Empowerment, New York, New York

An innovative effort to help low-income people save and better manage their money is a centerpiece of an ambitious antipoverty initiative in the nation's largest city.

IN JANUARY 2006, shortly after winning a second term in office, New York City Mayor Michael Bloomberg declared a new priority in his State of the City address. "Today, I am committing to a major reduction in the number of children, women, and men who live in poverty in this city over the next four years," he said. Richard Parsons, chief executive officer of Time Warner, and Geoffrey Canada, president and chief executive officer of the Harlem Children's Zone, would cochair a task force "to develop and implement our strategy, identify the most important measurements, and make sure that we refuse to accept failure," Bloomberg announced.[12]

Two of OFE's hallmark initiatives for eligible New York City residents are NYC Free Tax Prep, which provides free tax preparation, and NYC Financial Empowerment Centers, which provide free financial counseling. Pictured is a campaign ad that ran in 2014. *NYC Department of Consumer Affairs*

Eight months later, the mayor announced a set of policies and programs funded by $150 million in city money and philanthropic contributions. "The effort is classic Bloomberg in that it emphasizes nontraditional solutions and enlists the private sector to tackle problems that have historically vexed governments," the *New York Times* reported.[13] The city established the Center for Economic Opportunity (CEO) to support and coordinate activities across multiple city agencies, and over the next several years more than 30 programs were developed.

Evaluations of the initiative—which were substantially enhanced by the city's commitment to rigorous tracking of performance and impact—indicated that some programs that garnered the most initial attention fell short of their goals. Among these was a "family rewards" program that paid people for good behaviors, such as ensuring that their children went to school. Others, however, delivered results and have continued to this day. One of these is the Office of Financial Empowerment (OFE).

Equity Strategies, Results, and Challenges

The OFE was the first CEO program to become operational, opening for business in 2006 with the mission "to educate, empower, and protect low-income consumers in the financial services marketplace." It was housed in the city's Department of Consumer Affairs and from the outset viewed empowerment as consisting of both financial education and consumer protection. "It's not just an office of financial education; it's not just a small asset-building program," said Cathie Mahon, OFE's first executive director. "It is an office that has a comprehensive view: people need to be educated and they need to be empowered by getting access to a means of asset-building opportunities, but they also need to be protected."

OFE has rolled out an array of services and programs. Its current efforts include large-scale public awareness campaigns aimed at helping people save, manage, and protect their money. One example is the EITC Coalition Campaign, which helps poor working families realize the full benefits of the federal earned-income tax credit.[14] In 2015, the city said it helped about 145,000 people realize $250 million in refunds and savings through the program; it had ensured realization of more than $1 billion in EITC benefits through 2016.[15]

OFE's efforts are focused not just on expanding awareness of public benefits like the EITC and improving individuals' day-to-day financial management skills, but also on building family wealth through mechanisms such as low-cost and tax time–matched savings accounts and free employer-based checking accounts. And, reflecting its commitment to consumer protection, OFE offers services to help families with debt collection, sales of used cars, and tax preparation.

The office also provides free one-on-one financial counseling and connects families to other government agencies, nonprofit groups, and financial institutions that provide additional resources and assistance. With many of these partners, the OFE operates more than 30 financial empowerment centers, launched in 2008, to deliver services across New York City. The centers have

→

helped more than 25,000 people better manage their finances, pay down more than $14.7 million in debt, and build more than $2.4 million in savings. The centers originally were privately funded, but now are supported by the city in recognition of the fact that they are saving New York City money over the long term by reducing reliance on more expensive public benefits.[16]

The OFE's impact has spread far beyond New York City. In 2013, Bloomberg Philanthropies provided $16.2 million to the Living Cities' Cities for Financial Empowerment (CFE) Fund to offer grants to start centers for financial empowerment in Denver, Nashville, Philadelphia, San Antonio, and Lansing, Michigan, aiming to assist more than 30,000 people over three years. Nearly 50 cities had applied for the grants, and several that did not receive funding said they would attempt to establish centers with other resources.[17] In 2017, the CFE Fund, now its own 501(c) organization, reported that it had provided $25 million to assist more than 100,000 low-income people in 40 cities.[18]

When the Bloomberg administration created the OFE, the very idea that financial empowerment should be a major part of an antipoverty program was novel. As an evaluation by the Center for an Urban Future noted:

> Previously, there had been little acknowledgment that low assets, high debt, and lack of basic financial knowledge contributed to the cycle of poverty. Although the city has long had an alphabet soup of antipoverty programs, it had never embraced financial-literacy education and counseling as part of these efforts. Although a number of nonprofits focused on some aspects of financial literacy, such as teaching clients how to make a budget, OFE went a step further, providing one-on-one financial counseling and advising services.[19]

The OFE describes the broad-based benefits of its approach as a "super-vitamin" that not only improves the lives of the poor, but also makes other public programs on which they depend more effective, "improving the outcomes of traditional social service programming . . . [on a] better, faster, and less costly" basis.[20] While that thesis is still being tested, financial empowerment appears to remain a central part of the efforts of a growing number of cities to increase opportunity.

the value of providing financial advice when individuals are seeking city services. By leveraging a teachable moment, OFE coaches are able to encourage individuals to consider better, more productive financial decisions and improve their savings and payment behaviors over time.

Workforce and Skills Development

Cities have long understood the importance of workforce development programs for ensuring that employers have an adequate supply of trained workers. By preparing individuals for higher-paying jobs, such programs also contribute to the individuals' financial well-being and quality of life. But many traditional workforce programs have resulted in entry-level placements with little evidence that employees kept their jobs or advanced in them, forcing cities to rethink how workforce systems can truly spur economic mobility for local workers.

One fundamental challenge for cities has been how to get workforce systems that have focused primarily on job placement to evolve into systems that focus on ongoing skills development and advancement and that have a built-in equity component. Shifts in the labor market and advances in technology underscore the value of having workforce systems maintain a connection with education and job training, because jobs that offer sustaining wages require education and training that go beyond high school.

In order to develop a workforce system that successfully promotes equity and regional growth, cities should start by identifying their key growth sectors and the corresponding skills needed to fill the jobs of the future. City leaders then should analyze the gap between their current workforce and the skills required, as well as barriers that specific vulnerable populations face to entering the sector. (An example of this kind of approach can be found at "New Skills at Work," a Chicago skills gap report.[21])

A promising evidence-based approach that follows this general guidance is called *career pathways* and involves the following core elements:

- **PARTNERSHIP.** Partnerships—between employers in growth sectors identified by the city and providers of education and training—are designed to identify specific training needs for specific job openings in a particular field. Career pathways can focus on manufacturing, specific health care fields (such as medical office or direct patient care), information technology, or many other fields.

- **IDENTIFICATION OF A CAREER.** To facilitate progress toward progressively higher-skill and higher-paid jobs within a specific sector, a career pathway is established with multiple entrance and exit points that enable individuals to train for one position, work for a while, and then train for the next job on the path, taking small career steps at whatever pace works for that person.

- **CONTEXTUALIZED INSTRUCTION IN BASIC SKILLS.** This instruction focuses on preparing a person for work in a particular field (rather than providing general basic education) and on a structured pathway through education and training that helps that person stay on track toward qualifying for a particular job (rather than providing an unstructured community college curriculum that may be hard to navigate). These types of focused approaches can help significantly increase course completion rates.[22]

Another promising approach is *work-based learning*. Incorporating opportunities for participants to gain experience in their field through internships or job shadowing has proved valuable in preparing people for careers. Apprenticeships are especially promising because this approach combines all the above elements. Apprenticeships are designed by employers and often offer a progression of on-site and classroom learning.

The Carreras en Salud case study documents efforts by a community-based Chicago organization, Instituto del Progreso Latino, to prepare people for jobs in health care through a career pathways approach.

Carreras en Salud, Chicago, Illinois

A community-based organization creates career opportunities for low-income Latinos and helps meet the growing need for a bilingual health care workforce.

IN JUNE 2015, a JPMorgan Chase & Co. report titled "Growing Skills for a Growing Chicago" revealed a mismatch in the Chicago metro area between the number of "middle-skill" jobs—those requiring a high school degree and technical training but not a bachelor's degree—and the number of residents

The first Carreras en Sud cohort, 2005. *Instituto del Progreso Latino*

in the region who had the education and training to qualify for them. "If not addressed, this mismatch between job-seeker skills and business needs could hurt the region's economic competitiveness and limit the financial well-being of hundreds of thousands of people in the Chicago area," the report warned.[23]

Chicago, like many prosperous cities, is heavily dependent on middle-skill workers. They account for 44 percent of the region's workforce, the report found, and nearly 1 million of Chicago's middle-skill jobs—23 percent of the total—pay a median hourly wage of nearly $27. The jobs are in industries central to Chicago's future—health care, transportation, and manufacturing—and, according to the report, the region would add nearly 28,000 such jobs annually over the following five years.

"These are the jobs that are within reach of folks who for whatever reason find themselves in the lower-skilled areas right now," said Juan Salgado, president and chief executive officer of Instituto del Progreso Latino.[24] That organization, which Salgado has led since 2001, works with low-income, Latino immigrant communities on Chicago's South and West sides. Among its array of innovative programs, which in aggregate serve more than 14,000 people each year, is Carreras en Salud (Careers in Health), a promising effort aimed at creating opportunities in nursing, addressing precisely a shortage identified in the JPMorgan Chase report.

Equity Strategies, Results, and Challenges

Carreras en Salud was launched in 2005 as a collaboration among Instituto del Progreso Latino, the Association House of Chicago, the Humboldt Park Vocational Education Center of Wilbur Wright College, and the National Council of La Raza. The program has the twofold goal of helping lower-income people enter the nursing field and meeting a huge need for bilingual nursing care in Chicago. Latinos made up 25 percent of the city's population but less than 2 percent of its licensed practical and registered nurses.[25]

The program filled an important void in the local workforce development system. An analysis by Abt Associates noted: "While the Chicago metropolitan area offers a diverse range of training options outside of Instituto, the general pathway for low-skilled students who cannot enter directly into [certified nursing assistant] or [licensed practical nursing] training is to enroll in a standard, stand-alone ESL [English as a second language] course or in basic skills courses, which are not likely to provide the contextualized instruction or strong support that Carreras provides."[26]

Carreras targets adult Latinos throughout the Chicago metro area who have few or pre-college basic skills and are interested in nursing. To be eligible, individuals must have an annual family income of less than $35,000 and English literacy at the fourth-grade level or above.

Program participants receive instruction and support in reading, writing, and math; clinical practice in recognized health care facilities; and academic preparation to take the nursing boards state test and become licensed to work as a nurse or nurse assistant. Instituto also provides academic advice and tutoring, transportation assistance, and job placement services upon completion of training. Child care is provided to registered students, which is especially important for program participants, Instituto says, because about 60 percent of them care for their children independently.

As of the end of 2015, about 500 students had become licensed practical nurses, 400 more had become certified nurse assistants, and more than 200 were enrolled in the program. "Once they're licensed nurses, 100 percent of them get a job," earning $24 an hour or more, up from $10 an hour or less before they entered the program, Salgado said.[27]

The Carreras program reflects a career pathways approach. According to the Administration for Children and Families at the U.S. Department of Health and Human Services, such programs "provide postsecondary education and training that is organized as a series of manageable steps leading to successively higher credentials and employment opportunities in growing occupations."[28]

The idea is that each step along the career pathway provides greater skills and a credential valued in the job market that enables participants to grow in their careers and earn more money over time. A key principle is to mix and match the necessary education, training, and support services to each individual according to her or his needs and career progress. The career pathways approach depends heavily on close working relationships among employers—who identify high-priority needs and training requirements and ultimately hire trained individuals—providers of the training, and workforce agencies at the city and regional levels.

Though Carreras has produced overwhelmingly positive results and has gradually grown, it faces financial barriers to scale that are common among comprehensive career pathways programs. A National Council of La Raza report on Carreras noted: "It has been highlighted several times in this study that career pathway models require deep pockets of funding. The program has lofty goals of serving more students in the Chicago area, which will create capacity issues under the current management structure. The needs of the program's target population are deeper and more involved than the traditional college population."[29]

Instituto has both increased and diversified Carreras' funding. When the program began, it was funded entirely by small local foundations; today, the revenue base is an equal mix of private and public dollars.[30] This is an important sign that the program is meeting employers' needs. As more businesses in Chicago understand how effectively programs like Carreras can help fill jobs on which they and their region's success depends, more investment may follow, enabling promising programs to achieve greater impact.

Though the case study focuses on a particular local initiative, it is important to remember that job markets are regional: workforce development initiatives can benefit from collaboration among central cities and other municipalities in the broader region. In Chicago, for example, the city and Cook County have established the Chicago Cook Workforce Partnership to identify opportunities to align workforce development programs to meet the needs of residents and businesses in the region.

Small Business Development

According to the U.S. Small Business Administration,[31] small businesses are responsible for 66 percent of net new job creation since the 1970s. Small businesses also provide a critical asset-building opportunity and path to financial independence for small-business owners and their children.

While many cities have programs designed to support the growth of small businesses, most have not developed a cohesive data-driven strategy to expand their small businesses that is grounded in the local context. More research is needed to identify best practices and understand the economic networks that connect small, medium, and large businesses, including their interdependence on raw materials, talent, supply chains, and regulatory environment. But even as this research is conducted, there is much cities can do to create systems that support the growth of small businesses in general, and small businesses owned by people of color in particular.

This section first examines why cities should care about their local and regional small businesses and then looks at the challenges small businesses face and what cities can do to address them.

WHY CITIES SHOULD CARE ABOUT SMALL BUSINESSES

There are three main reasons why cities should focus on small business development. First, in most cities, small businesses create the majority of new jobs. A recent report by the JPMorgan Chase Institute and the Initiative for a Competitive Inner City (ICIC) found that businesses with five to 249 employees created most of the jobs in four of the five cities studied. Among businesses of this size, the greatest number of new jobs were produced by business on the high end of this spectrum.[32] Once businesses exceed 250 employees, they still create jobs but not at the same rate as during their scale-up phase.

Second, small businesses are more likely than other businesses to employ people of color and inner-city residents. The JPMorgan Chase Institute/ICIC report, for example, found that in four of the five cities examined, small businesses employed a greater share of inner-city residents than did large businesses. Other research has shown that small businesses owned by minorities are more likely to hire people of color.[33] Small businesses owned by racial or ethnic minorities can also help people of color build wealth, which can have an important independent effect in promoting economic mobility. Though some small businesses may be adding employees in relatively small numbers, the fact that they are hiring people facing higher barriers to employment is meaningful for improving economic mobility. While more research is needed to verify this hypothesis, some researchers suspect that small businesses may be more flexible regarding such traditional barriers to employment as an arrest record and poor credit.

Third, small businesses play a critical role in revitalizing neighborhoods and creating vibrant communities. Not only do small businesses help create desirable, destination neighborhoods, but they also provide local employment, often to minorities and members of low-income households in struggling communities. This was a major consideration when JPMorgan Chase joined the W.K. Kellogg Foundation and the Detroit Development Fund (DDF) to launch the Entrepreneurs of Color Fund in late 2015. Through the fund, a total of $7 million was committed to support Detroit-based neighborhood businesses owned by entrepreneurs of color and businesses that, without discriminating, tend primarily to hire people of color. In about 18 months, DDF deployed more than $4 million to 50 small business owners, 44 of which are located in neighborhoods trying to make a comeback.

Detroit is challenging many traditional notions of how community development works. The typical approach to revitalizing an area is to start with housing development that brings foot traffic and shoppers to a community, with small businesses following to meet the new demand. Detroit's West Village neighborhood is an example of the opposite approach: new retail businesses anchored the revitalization strategy, and new apartment units followed soon afterward.

BARRIERS FACED BY SMALL BUSINESSES

It is easy to tell a good news story about small-business success, but small-business owners face serious challenges. These obstacles are particularly acute for businesses owned by entrepreneurs of color and those with little inherited wealth. Four key challenges faced by small businesses are:

- **LITTLE CASH ON HAND.** In the report it released with ICIC, JPMorgan Chase Institute found that half the small businesses observed have less than a month's worth of cash on hand. With relatively small cash reserves, small businesses are very sensitive to local economic conditions, have difficulty working around prolonged payment schedules (for example, it can take 45 to 60 days to receive payment on an invoice on a government or construction contract), and can have difficulty stocking up supplies to meet a big order or prepare for a major contract opportunity. These obstacles present a barrier to growth.

- **EMPLOYMENT FLUCTUATIONS.** While small businesses are an important source of employment, the JPMorgan Chase Institute/ICIC report found that small businesses experience high fluctuations in employment—both increases and declines. This was especially true for young companies.

- **WORKFORCE SKILLS.** Once a small business is ready to scale up, the owners often report difficulty finding the right employees. Often small businesses are not aware that nonprofit training providers are available to help them identify and hire skilled workers. Even when they are aware of these services, according to a forthcoming report from the Center for Urban Innovation, local workforce training organizations may not provide the right incentives to encourage small businesses to hire locally because such businesses hire infrequently and may require tailored services that are difficult for training organizations to meet on demand. A related problem is that many owners of small businesses themselves lack the necessary management skills to effectively expand their businesses.

- **SHORTAGE OF CAPITAL.** A shortage of various kinds of capital can also be a major barrier to growth, particularly for African American and Hispanic businesses, which tend to be smaller and have lower revenues. Small businesses find themselves in a catch-22: they cannot gain access to the capital needed to expand their business, and the lack of revenue growth prevents them from being able to obtain investment capital. The number of Community Development Finance Institution (CDFI) Funds providing reasonably priced loans for those unable to qualify for a traditional bank loan has grown significantly over the past decade. However, a loan is not right for everyone. Few tools exist to help those who may need a more patient form of capital, such as equity. This, again, is a major barrier for individuals who have little wealth of their own and who cannot tap their friends and family network to raise the needed startup or scale-up capital.

Many small businesses also face barriers gaining access to support provided by cities and others that seek to help them. These barriers include:

- **POORLY COORDINATED SERVICES.** Services intended to support small businesses may be uncoordinated, unaligned, or misaligned with local growth industries or overlook certain sectors altogether. For example, cities often create tax incentives for large businesses and major employers and streamline ecosystems for startups, but leave retailers, restaurants, and supply-chain businesses to piece together assistance on their own.

- **CONFUSING, BURDENSOME REGULATIONS.** Regulations can be confusing or burdensome for small businesses, making it difficult to navigate the regulatory environment needed to succeed.

- **LACK OF A CITY STRATEGY.** Many cities lack a dedicated, cohesive strategy to aid small-business development, which can make it difficult for small businesses to find and gain access to the support they need and keep pace with changes in the support environment.

WHAT CITIES CAN DO TO SUPPORT SMALL BUSINESSES

Cities can help support the growth of small businesses in a number of ways. One important way is to use a data-driven approach to segment businesses and identify growth industries. As ICIC explains, the best small-business development strategies are not generic, but instead are customized to fit the assets and challenges faced by particular industry segments and markets. Cities can use the ICIC cluster mapping tool and playbook to help identify promising industry segments in their markets and then build public/private partnerships to identify and address the specific impediments holding back the growth of small businesses in those segments.[34]

Cities also can incorporate small businesses into their economic development strategy. In many cases, efforts to strengthen the vitality of specific neighborhoods go hand in hand with efforts to support the development of small businesses in those neighborhoods. Though a neighborhood-based approach is not the only approach to consider—as noted, it is also useful to focus on strengthening particular industry clusters—a focus on neighborhoods can be particularly useful for supporting the growth of businesses owned by minority and low-income residents. In Atlanta, for example, JPMorgan Chase has funded the Morehouse College Entrepreneurship Center to support the growth of women- and minority-owned small businesses in low-income neighborhoods through the Ascend 2020 project. Similarly, through the New Economy Initiative in Detroit, ten funders have come together to coordinate efforts to support entrepreneurship in Detroit and southeast Michigan.

As cities develop and execute neighborhood-based economic development strategies, it is important to consider the impact the success of such efforts may have on the ability of small businesses owned by minorities and others to continue to serve those neighborhoods. Just as gentrification can lead to the displacement of low-income residents from residential units, it can also lead to an increase in the rents for retail and office space, displacing local small businesses unable to afford higher rents. Explicit steps to keep rents affordable to local small businesses—and to provide new affordable retail and office space for such businesses—are an important part of managing neighborhood change.

Another approach to consider is directing a portion of the city's pension and other investments into venture capital funds and other investment vehicles that support the growth of minority-owned small businesses. Such funds help offset the challenges experienced by business owners who lack the ability to tap friends and family for funding to start and expand their businesses. Among other resources, such investors can be identified through the National Association of Investment Companies and the Altura Emerging Manager Database.

A final approach is to identify opportunities to reduce the paperwork and other red tape that often make it difficult for small businesses to

LiftFund, San Antonio, Texas

A loan fund serving small businesses and entrepreneurs adapts an internationally acclaimed microfinance model to deliver significant local benefits in the United States.

Myreida Salinas, owner of Myreida's Linens in Laredo, Texas, started her business with a LiftFund microloan in 2012. Through her relationship with LiftFund, Myreida has improved her credit score, expanded her business with a second loan, and increased her household income. *LiftFund*

ACCION INTERNATIONAL IS KNOWN WORLDWIDE for its leadership and innovation in microfinance, having lent nearly $8 billion—with a 97 percent repayment rate—to small entrepreneurs in more than 30 countries. Though perhaps best known for its efforts in Latin America, Africa, and Asia, the organization has had a U.S. presence since the early 1990s.

Accion opened a San Antonio office in 1994 and was quickly embraced by the city's business and political leadership, including Alfonso Martinez-Fonts, then chairman of the Greater San Antonio Chamber of Commerce and San Antonio president of Texas Commerce Bank. Among the early lenders and funders were Frost Bank, Wells Fargo, Broadway Bank, and Levi-Strauss. Accion's goal in San Antonio and other U.S. cities was consistent with its proven model in other countries: to support small businesses and entrepreneurs with no access to conventional capital sources and to bolster the economic self-sufficiency of low-income families and communities.

Under the name Accion Texas, the organization incorporated a nonprofit loan fund called LiftFund to deliver its products and services. Over time, it expanded to seven other cities in Texas and, starting in 2009, to other states. By 2015, Accion, through LiftFund, was serving 13 states throughout the South, Southwest, and California and had lent over $210 million to more than 17,000 small businesses. That same year, the organization formally changed its name to LiftFund while maintaining the same mission.

"LiftFund is more than a new name," former San Antonio mayor Henry Cisneros said when the change was made. "It is a launch into a new role, separate from Accion International. This entity will have its own momentum, its own drive, right out of San Antonio."[35] While LiftFund has continued to grow, the essence and effectiveness of its model can be seen best in its hometown.

Equity Strategies, Results, and Challenges

LiftFund's mission and approach are substantially similar to those of a microfinance organization operating overseas, with modifications that reflect small-business lending and the regulatory environment in the United States. "Borrowers of all types come to us," the lender's website says. "We lend to builders and hairdressers, auto shops, daycare centers, accounting firms, and staffing agencies, among others."[36]

Loans generally range in size from $500 to $1 million. (Lift Fund also makes loans up to $5.5 million, backed by the U.S. Small Business Administration, to help small businesses finance their commercial real estate and equipment needs.) Most borrowers use loan proceeds for essential working capital or equipment purchases.

The average credit score of a LiftFund borrower is 575, well below the threshold required by conventional small-business lenders. "Our focus [is] on helping or assisting small businessmen and women who don't have access to capital from traditional sources, like large financial institutions," says Adriana Biggs, the organization's chief strategy officer. "These individuals are people that, if not for LiftFund, have to go and borrow from payday lenders or

$\rightarrow$

title-loan establishments—predatory lenders where they are going to be paying 300 percent over the next four years. . . . We know that we're dealing with individuals who are ready to work—they have a business idea or a business in place—but all they need is access to capital."[37]

Even as LiftFund's activities and customers are atypical for a small-business lender, the organization has understood the importance of investing in systems and technologies similar to those used by conventional banks. For example, it uses an online loan processing platform that can categorize applications and assess risks in a matter of minutes, increasing efficiency and performance. "It's carving a good two days off of the loan origination," says Janie Barrera, LiftFund president and chief executive officer. "We wanted to develop a profile of a good paying customer and a not-so-good paying customer."[38]

A 2016 grant from JPMorgan Chase & Company is intended to help LiftFund in San Antonio and a number of other cities further employ technology to reduce loan approval time from an average of five weeks to an average of four days.[39]

LiftFund has long understood the importance of providing advice and assistance, as well as financing, to the entrepreneurs it supports. In 2014, LiftFund started operating Café Commerce, now known as Launch SA, which is billed as a one-stop shop for entrepreneurs "that blends technology, peer-to-peer mentorship, educational curriculum, and other programming and partnerships to make entrepreneurship easier, and speed the delivery and efficacy of small-business support resources."[40]

The organization in 2015 announced a partnership with the San Antonio Chamber of Commerce to provide small-business owners with intensive business training and mentoring aimed at building companies that can grow. Participants who complete the program will be eligible for a discounted loan for the business.[41]

LiftFund's impact in San Antonio alone has been significant. From 2010 to 2015, it made $23 million in loans in the city, with an average loan size of $3.9 million. The fiscal and economic impacts of LiftFund's lending during that period rippled beyond the borrowers, generating an estimated 2,147 jobs with an average wage of over $40,000, plus more than $87 million in income, $247 million in total economic impact, and $10 million in tax revenue.[42]

compete. Cities can do this, for example, by streamlining their procurement policies for smaller contracts to ensure that the administrative burden is manageable for small businesses. Cities also can work with anchor institutions and other businesses to encourage them to take similar steps to allow small businesses to be competitive. In Chicago, for example, anchor institutions are aligning their contracting policies and procedures so that once a small business qualifies at one location, it is certified to contract with all.

The LiftFund case study highlights how lenders can help small businesses by developing expertise in working with them and providing special products to meet their needs. Though LiftFund is not a city-led initiative, cities can help by supporting such entities as well as complementary strategies to help the small businesses they fund to grow.

Conclusion

The examples in this chapter illustrate only a few of the many creative approaches cities are taking to support economic mobility. Other city initiatives not included here include efforts to expand the availability of child care, implement universal or near-universal pre-K schooling, raise the minimum wage, and facilitate completion of college. For cities looking to deepen their role in helping individuals move up the economic ladder, an abundance of promising examples exist on which cities can base their own initiatives.

CHAPTER 5

Developing Strategic Plans

TO MAKE PROGRESS IN INCREASING ECONOMIC MOBILITY, a city needs to take multiple steps across a range of disciplines. One way to jump-start these efforts is to develop an economic mobility plan or equity plan that articulates a comprehensive strategy for advancing in these areas. The city also needs a mechanism for tracking and overseeing the implementation of these plans, coordinating the efforts of multiple city departments, and holding itself accountable for results. These efforts should be informed by robust public input, including through the creative use of technology to ensure that all voices are heard.

The first of this chapter's three sections discusses the impediments to progress that give rise to the need for sustained and strategic leadership by cities. The second section, based on an analysis of these challenges, provides recommendations for a strategic planning and implementation process that can help cities more effectively and holistically promote economic mobility. The chapter concludes with profiles of the mayors of Atlanta and Detroit, exploring how they have exercised leadership in promoting equity in their cities.

The Need for Sustained and Strategic Leadership by Cities

Efforts are underway in all U.S. cities to address the fundamental challenges inhibiting economic mobility and to help individuals move up the economic ladder. Despite these efforts, however, substantial barriers to economic mobility remain. To accelerate progress, cities need to develop a more integrated and strategic approach that responds to the shortcomings of the current system.

As a system for coherently addressing problems of inequality and gaps in access to opportunity, the existing framework of funding and executing a human services program has serious deficiencies. Among other challenges, most service-delivery programs operate independently of each other: each chooses its own area of concentration and specialization, with the result that there is little coordination to ensure comprehensive coverage of either residents' needs or the city's geographic area. Many individuals and families are left unserved.

Within both government and the nonprofit sector, services are generally delivered through silos according to the nature of federal funding streams, patterns and habits of specialization, and the local traditions of expertise of delivery organizations. They are not driven by comprehensive approaches to changing demographics, evolving economic circumstances, or the deep underlying needs of the urban poor.

Such delivery systems also ignore the nature of poverty itself, which can be addressed only through long-term commitment—even generational commitment—requiring organizational consistency to deliver services continually over a long period. Sadly, poverty is characterized by recidivism and human setbacks, and thus people trapped in poverty require intense, interpersonal attention. Unfocused, episodic, and discontinuous efforts are no match for the persistence of grinding poverty.

Many human services organizations are structured to take up problems as they arise—literally, to handle walk-in cases—which leaves them dealing with individuals who are not being helped by other services. Organizations acting alone are unable to provide a comprehensive response to the complex problems experienced by low-income individuals, families, and communities.

The scale of poverty in cities is generally very large, and addressing it requires a system that is up to the task of handling problems on this scale. The issue of scale is exacerbated by the constant flow of new individuals into poverty. The combination of job losses, family dysfunction, drug addiction, young people dropping out of school, and people reaching the frailty of old age creates a constant stream of entrants on the poverty rolls and swells the challenges facing cities.

These realities suggest it is necessary to confront the larger context of poverty, which is interwoven with a series of larger urban dynamics—urban economies whose high-skill jobs are often a mismatch for the skills of those living in poverty; workers displaced as companies downsize or move away; lack of affordable housing, which results in evictions and increases homelessness; lower wages as workers are displaced by technology; and elderly residents whose inadequate retirement savings fall short of health care costs. The result is a context of rapid change that overwhelms the separate efforts of individual antipoverty organizations.

Exacerbating these challenges is inadequate funding, particularly when funds are disbursed thinly, unpredictably, and inconsistently across poverty problems that are inherently the opposite—deep, predictable, and consistent and persistent. Federal funding is being reduced, local governments face deficits, and public support is being undercut by evidence of widening divides between the poor and the prosperous.

These deficiencies in the disjointed system of offering services undermine the ability of the nation to organize a comprehensive attack on inequality. The national dialogue of recent years concerning widening income inequality raises profound concerns about whether the nation's present effort is up to the task. The federal government seems increasingly incapable of action due to budget deficits and debt projections and is gridlocked to the point that programs with new ideas commensurate with current poverty levels cannot be enacted. Moreover, the federal commitment to equity seems frozen by philosophical disagreements concerning the role of government itself. State governments, which generally have not been leaders on the equity agenda, are confronted with their own budget shortfalls that limit their capacity to assume a larger role.

Meanwhile, cities are the focal point of the diverse populations struggling in the new economy. Cities, therefore, are squarely involved in the debate about inequality. Whether or not they want to lead the nation's equity agenda, cities are places where the inequality is acute and therefore where action is demanded.

As stated by San Antonio Mayor Ron Nirenberg, who established equity as the theme of his first budget: "Unfairness stemming from San Antonio's early growth patterns has shortchanged some areas of town across several generations.... This inequity cannot be ignored. It must be addressed.... Equity is implementing the promises that politicians make to voters when they walk around neighborhoods and tell residents they deserve better."[1]

Developing and Implementing a Strategic Approach

As noted in the Henry Cisneros preface, cities are the logical leaders of efforts to help families advance economically. They are on the front lines and in the best position to understand the makeup of poverty in their communities. They need not be the initiator of services in every case or the sole provider of resources, but they can frame the context and create a network of action to engage existing organizations and streams of funding, and weave the efforts into a coherent response. Also, as institutions with permanence, cities have the capability to establish the kinds of long-term measures needed to tackle poverty and inequality.

To make substantial progress in increasing economic mobility, cities need to address the problems exhibited by existing service-delivery systems. This means developing an integrated approach that both facilitates coordination among service-delivery organizations and breaks down the silos that lead to service duplication and inefficiency, allowing people to fall between the cracks of narrowly defined social programs. Cities need to move from a focus on providing *services* to a focus on investing in *systems* that help people overcome challenges that keep them from realizing their economic potential. Cities also need to think creatively and comprehensively about the many ways they can capitalize on their existing activities to advance equity objectives. If a city needs land to provide affordable housing, it can consider developing the housing on unused or underused city-owned property. If a city is looking for a way to help residents build financial capability, it can add financial coaching to the services included in existing social service interactions.

In short, cities need to make economic mobility a top priority, then take a strategic approach that facilitates coordination, alignment, integration, and expansion of existing services to more effectively meet residents' needs. This approach should be grounded in a strategic plan that defines the city's goals, describes how the city plans to achieve them, and includes quantitative targets that allow the city—and the public—to measure progress. This plan can be an *economic mobility plan*, focused specifically on place-based and people-based approaches to promoting economic mobility, or an *equity plan*, focused on a broader set of objectives that includes these approaches but also covers some or all of the additional components of the equity agenda.

Rather than include the details of all the social service systems that influence economic mobility or equity, a city's economic mobility plan or equity plan should operate at a higher level. It should focus on the transformative strategies the city intends to implement to really move the dial, plus the overall metrics the city will use to gauge its progress, cross-referencing subject-specific plans that include more details on specific strategies within each area.

For example, as discussed in Chapter 3, a city should develop a comprehensive local housing strategy that describes how it will use all the many tools at its disposal to meet its housing objectives. Similarly, most school districts should have an education plan that describes how the district plans to improve education outcomes. These subject-specific plans should provide the detail that justifies the high-level strategies incorporated in the economic mobility plan or equity plan. Compiling all these subject-specific plans into a single volume would only serve to create an unwieldy tome and would not advance the goal of increased economic mobility and equity.

In developing their plans, cities should be mindful of the capacity of local nonprofits and government agencies. Many of the necessary program models are challenging to execute and likely to be successful only when implemented by high-performing organizations. A successful strategy may well need to focus both on the adoption of effective program models and the cultivation of high-performing nonprofit organizations and government agencies to administer them.

Of course, there are plans, and then there are *plans*. Many plans are developed to meet the requirements of the state or federal government. Often, these plans are well intentioned and include a lot of useful information, but they are not really strategic in the sense that they identify goals that truly drive decision making and describe a strategy that has a realistic chance of making measurable progress toward solving a problem. To be effective, a strategic plan needs to articulate a real strategy that leads to realignment of the programmatic infrastructure, shifts in funding to programs that will help the city make faster progress toward its goals, and regular monitoring of data to assess whether the strategy is working and what changes are needed to ensure that it is effective in producing the desired outcomes.

Rather than simply summarize a city's existing programs in a new format, an economic mobility plan or equity plan should challenge the status quo. Among other questions, the developers of the plan should ask: Are we doing enough in each area to achieve our equity goals? If not, how can we expand or shift our efforts to have more impact? In which areas can new investments generate the biggest impacts? How can we do things differently to better align existing systems and resources to achieve shared goals?

The plan also needs to be implemented by individuals with the authority to get things done. Ideally, the development and implementation of the plan would be overseen by a high-ranking city official with the power to require the programmatic changes needed to better align existing systems as well as the funding shifts needed to support the strategy. Regular meetings of the many city agencies that play a role in implementing programs that are part of the strategy are essential. These meetings should include not only departments of city government, but also other public or quasi-public agencies that implement relevant programs, such as the local housing authority and the independent school district. Ideally, these meetings would both inform the development of the strategy and track implementation of the recommended approaches. The efforts should also be informed by regular interaction with one or more advisory groups composed of representatives from service-delivery organizations, philanthropic foundations, business leaders, community-based organizations, and other stakeholders.

Some cities, such as Atlanta and Austin, have established the position of chief equity officer. Depending on how the position is constituted, the chief equity officer can provide a helpful structure for coordinating a city's equity efforts. One question to ask in creating or reviewing such a position is whether the equity officer has sufficient power to shape the way systems are aligned and budget decisions are made. If not, it is important either to vest the position with this power or to assign a high-ranking official, such as a deputy mayor, to oversee the equity planning process. In the latter scenario, the chief equity officer would play an essential, complementary role to that of the deputy mayor, overseeing the implementation of the equity plan, coordinating the information needed among the different departments, and making recommendations to the deputy mayor on programmatic and budget shifts needed to accomplish the plan's goals.

Another approach to the equity officer position is to give it less of a "line position" and make it more an office that keeps the mayor and city council informed regarding the progress of equity efforts, using metrics that bring measurement, accountability, and discipline to the system. The concept would be akin to the budgetary scoring role provided for the U.S. Congress by the Congressional Budget Office.

Cities also need robust mechanisms for obtaining public input. Ideally, cities would combine traditional mechanisms—such as town hall meetings, neighborhood meetings, and other public forums—with the creative use of technology. Des Moines, Iowa, for example, used the Design My DSM interactive tool to obtain public input on the city's planning priorities. Users of the tool could rank their priorities for the future, learn about potential planning projects, and indicate which projects they would choose to fund with a limited budget. Similarly, Knoxville, Tennessee, used the online application MetroQuest to allow users to weigh in on their priorities for the future and explore potential growth scenarios. Knoxville paired this technology with more traditional in-person outreach, offering local groups all the materials they needed to hold a local planning discussion through a "meeting in a box."[2]

Finally, cities need a mechanism for tracking and overseeing implementation of their plans, coordinating the efforts of multiple city departments, and holding themselves accountable for results. The regular meetings of department heads, as described earlier—with the active oversight of a deputy mayor or other high-ranking official—can provide the infrastructure for internal tracking of progress and ensuring that the requisite collaboration and coordination are taking place.

Though those attending these meetings should consider data on outcomes to determine whether the city is on track to meet its goals, the accountability system will be most effective if the data are shared publicly on a regular basis. The data should be accompanied by an analysis of the areas in which the city has been most and least successful, and an explanation of the changes needed to the economic mobility plan or equity plan in order to achieve the desired results. This calls for, at a minimum, annual public reporting on accomplishments and progress toward benchmarks, along with periodic updating—perhaps every three years—of the plan itself.

The development, implementation, and monitoring of a truly transformative strategic plan to advance economic mobility or equity is a major undertaking far beyond the capacity of any one individual. Ideally, the person charged with overseeing the plan would have access to a department capable of collecting and analyzing data, reviewing the plans of individual agency heads to determine the changes needed to better align plans, and evaluating programs to determine their impact. The Mayor's Office for Economic Opportunity in New York City provides one model for this function. Originated as a commission investigating potential approaches for promoting economic mobility, the office has grown into a city agency that conducts research and program evaluations; designs new programs and consults on improvements in existing programs; collects data on key equity outcomes, including for an enhanced poverty measure; and integrates data across departments.

Profiles of Atlanta and Detroit

While the development and implementation of an economic mobility plan or equity plan can provide an important framework for making progress, it is less an end in and of itself than a mechanism for implementing the broader recommendation that cities elevate economic mobility as a top priority and take a strategic approach to advancing it. The authors are unaware of any U.S. city that has acted as comprehensively and holistically as recommended here to advance economic mobility or equity. But many have made substantial progress. The two mayors profiled here have elevated equity objectives significantly in their administrations, each in his own way.

Among his many accomplishments as mayor of Atlanta, Kasim Reed appointed the city's first chief equity officer, developed the Comprehensive Center for Fathers, and obtained public approval for higher taxes to

Mayor Kasim Reed

TAKING OFFICE IN 2010 as mayor of Atlanta—a job he had aspired to since he was 13—Kasim Reed realized his first great challenge was to rebuild the city's finances and restore the capital markets' confidence that Atlanta would remain among the ranks of premier American cities for investment.

Atlanta Mayor Kasim Reed. *Rick Diamond/ Getty Images*

After significant success on those fronts, reflected in measures such as an annually balanced budget and steadily improving bond ratings, Reed spent much of his second term trying to ensure that Atlanta's economic successes would not exacerbate longstanding disparities in income and opportunity—and instead could be a basis for healing them.

In 2016, Reed, told a local reporter, "It's in our interest right now to turn to equity. If we address this now, we'll assure that we will become one of the leading cities in the world."[3] Reed later described the challenges of income inequality and lack of opportunity for some Atlantans as "asymmetric threats to our future prosperity."[4]

Reed's response to these challenges cuts across multiple areas of municipal responsibility and, perhaps not surprisingly in a city infamous for traffic congestion, includes a major commitment to transit. "[Transit] is about equity," he told *Atlanta* magazine. "It's about a fair shot and a fair shake and people being about to use transit. But I'm here to make the argument that equity is profitable."[5]

Reed made a concerted case for voter approval of tax increases to fund long-needed transit investments. In November 2016, a half-cent sales tax referendum on a $2.6 billion Metropolitan Atlanta Regional Transit Authority (MARTA) expansion passed with 71 percent approval. Another measure that will raise an estimated $300 million for infrastructure projects passed with 68 percent support.

To mobilize voters, Reed touted recent corporate headquarters relocations to Atlanta by NCR, Honeywell, GE Digital, UPS, and EquiFax, which he argued were driven in part by MARTA's reputation for good service. But, as Reed said in his 2016 State of the City address, "It's not enough to see companies set up shop here if we don't also set up the next generation for success."[6]

Housing is another area where Reed has driven market-based policies designed to tap Atlanta's hot real estate market to expand opportunity. His administration's Workforce Housing Policy provides that developers receiving direct funding or incentives from the city must make 10 to 15 percent of residential units in their projects affordable for lower- and middle-income households.

The Anti-Displacement Tax Fund is a newly created vehicle to help ensure that current homeowners are not priced out of rapidly gentrifying Westside neighborhoods. The fund is designed to provide grants to homeowners to offset property tax increases so they can remain in their neighborhoods as real estate values rise—as they have by nearly 40 percent in the past four years. The fund is capitalized by a combination of city, corporate, and philanthropic sources.

Reed's interest in inclusion is reflected in other areas as well. His administration touts its efforts to boost minority- and women-owned businesses, for example, and to support families through the Comprehensive Center for Fathers, which is aimed at young men, and extended paid parental leave for mothers and primary caregivers.

Reed sees Atlanta's current efforts to be a more inclusive city as a natural extension of its history as the cradle of the U.S. civil rights movement. Though his administration has not developed a formal plan that encompasses its various initiatives, Reed did create the position of chief equity officer for the city and hired for the position Royce Brooks, who reports directly to him. "Her job is to constantly challenge my administration on whether we are being fairer and more equitable."[7]

Even as Reed neared the end of his term-limited eight years as mayor, he worked to share his city's lessons with others. In November 2016, the National League of Cities (NLC) announced that Reed would chair the new NLC Task Force on Economic Mobility and Opportunity. Composed of 22 local leaders from across the country, the task force over the next year "will identify recommendations for cities to address economic barriers that are keeping many families from sharing in our country's prosperity," NLC said.[8]

support transportation improvements that will improve connectivity in all Atlanta neighborhoods. The mayor's appointee for chief equity officer, Royce Brooks, has provided constant reminders of the need to integrate equity goals into all city efforts. One example is Brooks's effort to prevent homeowners in Atlanta's Westside neighborhoods from being displaced by rising property taxes. By raising funding from a range of sources to cover the taxes associated with increased assessments, Brooks was able to assure residents that their taxes would not go up for 20 years, helping ensure that they would benefit as local conditions in the neighborhood improve.

Mayor Mike Duggan of Detroit takes a different approach to elevating equity. Rather than focusing on the subject through the lens of race or income, he strives to achieve equity for longstanding residents—more than 80 percent of whom are African American—who have stayed with the city despite many challenging years. All too often residents living in gentrifying neighborhoods end up being priced out of their housing just as the neighborhood improves. Though Detroit does not have the same kinds of gentrification pressures as those faced by high-cost cities like New York or San Francisco, the high poverty rate in the city leaves residents vulnerable to even modest changes in rents. Many Detroit residents are worried that the major investments being made in the city's turnaround will lead to rent and home price increases that will make it difficult for them to stay in the city. Duggan came back to this point again and again during an interview with the authors, emphasizing the fundamental importance of doing right by longtime residents.

Though Reed and Duggan take very different approaches, both have made achievement of more-equitable outcomes a high priority for their administrations. In a country as diverse as the United States, it is not surprising that multiple paths will exist for elevating equity goals and making economic mobility a key priority. Each city will need to find the path that best fits its assets, its challenges, and its regional context.

Mayor Mike Duggan

FOR MAYOR MIKE DUGGAN, Detroit's continuing comeback is about rebuilding the city for the people who stayed during the decades of disinvestment that shrank the population by more than a million residents and the traumatic bankruptcy from which the city emerged in 2014.

While fully focused on ensuring that the city he runs can deliver basic services, Duggan is also mindful of the displacement pressures than can accompany redevelopment. "We're trying to rebuild Detroit for those who stayed during the recovery so they can see a future for themselves here," he said.[9]

Jobs are a top priority for Duggan. The unemployment rate was down to 7.5 percent as of July 2017, the lowest level since 2000. Duggan says his efforts "have a lot of layers."[10]

Detroit Mayor Mike Duggan. *City of Detroit*

One layer is the Detroit at Work website and referral program. Developed in close collaboration with Detroit employers, the program aims to link residents with available jobs—in occupations ranging from food service to asbestos removal—through training programs that have a direct pipeline to those jobs. Duggan is also working with labor unions to get more Detroit residents hired onto local construction projects.

Duggan is especially proud of his administration's efforts to provide jobs to newly released prisoners in fields where Detroit businesses need workers, such as environmental cleanup, culinary arts, and forklift operation. As he told the *Detroit Free Press*, "We went and looked at where employers were hiring right now. . . . If Detroit's comeback is going to be successful, we need everybody's talents, and this is a way to make sure we use the talents of people who have paid their debt."[11]

Another dimension of Duggan's pragmatic, jobs-driven approach to making Detroit more inclusive is his support for a 2016 ordinance—the first of its kind in the country—that requires developers of projects receiving city funding and subsidies to negotiate a package of job opportunities and other benefits for surrounding neighborhoods. The requirements, which apply to projects

→

with an investment of at least $75 million seeking city subsidies of at least $1 million, are intended to be legally binding and subject to regular public reporting.

Neighborhood revitalization is a top priority as well. For Duggan and Detroit, it starts with remediating blight. The city has demolished nearly 12,000 vacant and dangerous structures since January 2014—evidence showed that modest property value increases in occupied homes nearby—and planned to do the same during another two-year period. Duggan's administration also has resold thousands of the houses it took for failure to pay taxes to owners who have either refurbished them or torn them down for conversion to community space.

Duggan also has championed the idea of "20-minute neighborhoods"— revitalized areas where residents can meet all their basic needs through a short walk or bike ride. The concept serves as the basis for an intensive set of investments—in housing, green space, and infrastructure—in targeted parts of neighborhoods with high levels of vacancy.

The concept is being piloted in the Fitzgerald neighborhood, near the University of Detroit Mercy and Marygrove College. A recently announced revitalization plan will invest more than $4 million in the rehab of 115 vacant homes, create a new two-acre Ella Fitzgerald Park, and landscape 192 vacant lots. Six other neighborhoods have been identified for similar investments.

Understandable for a mayor committed to bringing back Detroit for families who have hung in through tough times, Duggan is focused on schools, even though he has limited ability to control them. The city and the school board are working together to convince the state not to close lower-performing schools without considering the impact on children.

"We have 110,000 schoolchildren in this city, which means we need 110,000 seats in quality schools," he said in his 2017 State of the City address. "Closing a school doesn't add a quality seat. All it does is bounce our children around from place to place. Before you close a school, you need to make sure there's a better alternative."[12]

Conclusion

Among the most difficult dilemmas in American history have been those associated with concepts of equality, fairness, opportunity, equity, social mobility, racial justice, class, and inclusion. The words themselves dredge up ancient battles that date to the origins of the republic and are no less contentious now.

America today is a more fair, open, and upwardly mobile society than ever before. But modern forces such as globalism, technology, demographics, and financial and economic shifts constantly create new realities. To keep national mechanisms of economic integration and social mobility current and relevant to these new realities, every contributing sector of society must adapt and assume new roles. That includes national and state governments, private businesses and nonprofits, churches and philanthropies, schools and colleges, and both traditional and social media.

In this metropolitan nation, it is in cities and urban areas where these sectors come together in their effort to improve equity. Perhaps now more than ever, in an era of notable city comebacks and breakthrough urban growth, the nation can harness the momentum of its cities, communities, and regions to ensure that we stay the course in our common journey toward a more perfect union.

Measures for Tracking Outcomes

BUILDING ON THE DISCUSSION IN CHAPTER 2, this appendix provides an overview of specific metrics cities can use to track the success or failure of their efforts to promote economic mobility. These measures fall into six categories: income, educational achievement, financial health, affordable housing, racial and ethnic segregation, and neighborhood disparities.

Income

Cities successful in promoting economic mobility should experience increases in incomes among low-income households and racial and ethnic minorities, as well as reduced inequality of incomes.[1] These can be tracked with the following metrics.

- **PROGRESS BY POPULATIONS IN NEED.** To understand whether incomes are trending in the right direction for low-income households, cities can track the incomes of households in the bottom half of the income distribution. One measure is the average income for this group. Another is the income of households in a specific percentile of the distribution, such as the 25th percentile. Cities can also track the average income of members of racial and ethnic minorities. By looking at trends in these measures over time, as adjusted for inflation, cities can determine to what extent these population segments are making progress in attaining higher incomes.[2]

- **REDUCED INEQUALITY.** Income inequality is generally measured by the Gini coefficient. A reduction in the coefficient is a sign that wealth is being more evenly distributed and thus that income inequality has declined. To understand whether they are making progress in reducing income inequality, cities can track the Gini coefficient over time to see if it is declining, indicating a positive trend. Even a slowing of a trend toward higher Gini coefficients could be a sign of progress. Cities can also compare the average incomes of people of different races and ethnicities to examine the extent to which gaps narrow over time.

Educational Achievement

The question of whether and to what extent student test results should be used to measure the quality of individual schools is a matter of considerable debate. However a city or state chooses to measure school quality, it is important to examine the extent to which children of different incomes, races, and ethnicities have access to high-quality schools. It is also important to measure the extent to which children in low-income households and racial and ethnic minorities are improving their educational achievement.

Given the focus on student testing by the federal government through the No Child Left Behind Act (2002) and the Every Student Succeeds Act (2015), as well as the ongoing efforts of states and local governments, many cities already have sophisticated measures in place for tracking student achievement; where available, these measures can be used to track outcomes. The following examples illustrate the kinds of outcomes cities may want to consider in determining whether they are making progress toward more equitable educational outcomes.

■ **PROGRESS BY POPULATIONS IN NEED.** One approach is to track over time the average test scores for a group of low-income students, such as students eligible for a free or reduced-cost lunch. A city can also focus on changes in average test scores for racial or ethnic minorities. One issue to bear in mind is that test formats change, so it may be difficult in some areas to find comparable test results over an extended period. An alternative is to examine the share of low-income and minority students meeting minimum standards in reading and math. However, minimum standards also change over time, so the comparability of this measure must also be considered.[3]

- **REDUCED INEQUALITY.** Progress toward equitable education outcomes can be measured by tracking gaps in test scores by income, race, and ethnicity. Reductions in these gaps would be a sign of progress.

Financial Health

Progress in improving individuals' financial health can be tracked in a number of ways. Credit scores provide the most widely accessible measure, though a partnership with a credit bureau is needed to obtain such data. Another possible measure is the Financial Well-Being Scale developed in 2015 by the Consumer Finance Protection Bureau, though this would require a periodic survey to track changes over time.

- **PROGRESS BY POPULATIONS IN NEED.** One approach is to track changes over time in the average credit score for households in the bottom half of the income distribution. Though credit bureau data do not include directly reported data on income, the credit bureaus have algorithms for estimating income. Alternatively, or in addition, cities can track changes over time in the credit scores of racial and ethnic minorities. Average credit scores in census tracts with low incomes can also be tracked, though in this case, care should be taken to consider and control for shifts in demographics.

- **REDUCED INEQUALITY.** Progress in reducing inequality can be measured by tracking disparities in credit scores by income, race, and ethnicity. Reductions in these disparities would be a sign of progress toward more equitable outcomes.

Affordable Housing

The following are approaches for measuring increases in the affordability of housing in resource-rich areas.

- **PROGRESS BY POPULATIONS IN NEED.** To measure improvements in the affordability of housing in resource-rich areas, cities can track the share of housing affordable to very low-income households[4] in zip codes or census tracts with high-quality schools,[5] low rates of crime, and good access to jobs and public transit. Cities can also examine trends for households at other income levels. Communities may want to focus separately on trends for different opportunity indicators—such as schools, crime, job access, and public transit access—as well as for composite measures that combine data for multiple indicators into a single index.[6] Because many resource-rich areas are outside a city's boundaries—for example, suburban communities with good schools—it is important to measure this factor at both the local and regional levels.

- **REDUCED INEQUALITY.** Access to resource-rich areas may vary by race, ethnicity, and income. Cities can track their progress in reducing inequality in such access by measuring the percentages of people of different races, ethnicities, and incomes in the city and region who live in resource-rich areas. Inequality is reduced when gaps are reduced. As noted, cities may wish to focus both on individual dimensions of opportunity and on an aggregate index that includes multiple measures.

Racial and Ethnic Segregation

In regions with significant levels of segregation, efforts to expand the availability of affordable housing in amenity-rich areas should lead to reductions in racial and ethnic segregation. The following are approaches to measuring progress.

- **PROGRESS BY MINORITIES.** Cities can measure the extent to which members of racial and ethnic minorities are able to gain access to resource-rich integrated neighborhoods by tracking the percentage of the city's racial and ethnic minority households living in such neighborhoods. Each city may wish to develop its own threshold for defining resource-rich and integrated neighborhoods.

- **REDUCED INEQUALITY.** A common approach to measuring racial and ethnic segregation is to calculate a dissimilarity index showing the extent to which two groups—for example, African Americans and non-Latino whites, or Latinos and non-Latino whites—are evenly distributed across a geographical area. The U.S. Department of Housing and Urban Development's Affirmatively Furthering Fair Housing (AFFH) Data and Mapping Tool provides access to dissimilarity index data for cities, regions, and other jurisdictions.[7] This measure should also be tracked at both the city and regional levels.

Neighborhood Disparities

In addition to improved outcomes for individual households, efforts to address spatial inequities by strengthening the resources and amenities available in struggling neighborhoods should result in measurable reductions in neighborhood disparities.

- **PROGRESS BY POPULATIONS IN NEED.** Progress in this area can be measured by identifying one or more groups of neighborhoods of interest—for example, low-income neighborhoods or segregated neighborhoods—and examining the extent to which they experience improvements on key measures of neighborhood opportunity, such as school performance, crime, and transportation access.

- **REDUCED INEQUALITY.** To determine whether neighborhood disparities are growing or shrinking over time, the performance of low-income or segregated neighborhoods can be compared with that of higher-income or integrated neighborhoods in terms of key measures of opportunity, such as school performance, crime, and transportation access.

Notes

CHAPTER 2

1   While some cities may wish to focus on developing a plan for promoting economic mobility specifically, others may wish to broaden the process to promote equity more broadly. A broader process could include, for example, strategies identified in both columns of figure 1.

2   See Chris Benner and Manuel Pastor, *Equity, Growth, and Community: What the Nation Can Learn from America's Metro Areas* (Oakland, CA: University of California Press, 2015); Randall Eberts, George Erickcek, and Jack Kleinhenz, *Dashboard Indicators for the Northeast Ohio Economy: Prepared for the Fund for Our Economic Future,* Working Paper 06-05 (Cleveland: Federal Research Bank of Cleveland, 2008); Manuel Pastor, "Cohesion and Competitiveness: Business Leadership for Regional Growth and Social Equity," in *Competitive Cities in the Global Economy* (Paris: OECD Publishing, 2006); and Manuel Pastor, Peter Dreier, J. Eugene Grigsby III, and Marta Lopez-Garza, *Regions that Work: How Cities and Suburbs Can Grow Together* (Minneapolis: University of Minnesota Press, 2000).

3   Chris Benner and Manuel Pastor, *Equity, Growth, and Community: What the Nation Can Learn from America's Metro Areas* (Oakland, CA: University of California Press, 2015).

4   Eberts, Erickcek, and Kleinhenz, *Dashboard Indicators.*

5   Organisation for Economic Co-operation and Development (OECD) Directorate for Employment, Labour, and Social Affairs, "Does income inequality hurt economic growth?" *Focus on Inequality and Growth*, December 2014.

6   For a detailed account of the OECD findings on the relationship between income inequality and economic growth, see Organisation for Economic Co-operation and Development, *In It Together: Why Less Inequality Benefits All* (Paris: OECD Publishing, 2015).

7   Gregory Acs, Rolf Pendall, Mark Treskon, and Amy Khare, *The Cost of Segregation: National Trends and the Case of Chicago, 1990–2010* (Washington, DC: Urban Institute, March 2017).

8   Paul Jargowsky, *Architecture of Segregation: Civil Unrest, the Concentration of Poverty, and Public Policy* (New York: Century Foundation, 2015).

CHAPTER 3

1   Fair housing programs and literature often use the term *opportunity areas* to denote places targeted for the development of affordable housing (or for Housing Choice Voucher holders to lease) in order to maximize the access of families to place-based resources. Because the authors of this book believe cities should work to ensure that *all* neighborhoods become opportunity areas in the sense that they provide residents with the building blocks of economic opportunity, they have chosen to focus in this chapter on an alternative term—*resource-rich areas*. This terminology avoids the risk of suggesting that families must move to gain access to the resources they need in order to advance economically. It also recognizes that some areas currently provide more resources—better schools, safer streets, better access to jobs—and there is value in ensuring that households of all incomes have the ability to live in such resource-rich areas.

2   See the King County Housing Authority's *Moving to Work FY 2017 Annual Plan*, https://www.kcha.org/Portals/0/PDF/MTW/2017_MTW_Plan.pdf.

3   See the Opportunity Mapping toolkit, www.psrc.org/sites/default/files/opportunity_mapping.pdf, in the Puget Sound Regional Council's *Planning for Whole Communities Toolkit.*

4   Other policy objectives a city may seek to achieve through a comprehensive housing policy include, for example, ending chronic homelessness, expanding the supply of affordable housing in the jurisdiction, improving housing quality, protecting residents in gentrifying areas from displacement, helping residents achieve sustainable homeownership, and promoting healthy housing.

5   See the "Frequently Asked Questions" page on the Opportunity Moves website, http://opportunitymoves.org/faq.

6   The National Community of Practice on Local Housing Policy, a joint effort of the New York University Furman Center and Abt Associates, is funded by the Ford Foundation and the John D. and Catherine T. MacArthur Foundation.

7   Bob Gardner, Nimira Lalani, and Cristina Plamadeala, *Comprehensive Community Initiatives: Lessons Learned, Potential and Opportunities Moving Forward* (Toronto: Wellesley Institute for Advancing Urban Health, 2010).

8   Center for Promise, "Transforming East Lake: Systematic Intentionality in Atlanta," case study, www.americaspromise.org/sites/default/files/d8/APA_EastLake_C6_R5%5B1%5D.pdf.

9   Maya Brennan, "Improvements to Education—and Housing—Are Game Changers for Atlanta's Children," *Urban Land*, June 1, 2015, https://urbanland.uli.org/industry-sectors/improvements-education-housing-game-changers-atlantas-children.

10   Jill Khadduri, Heather Schwartz, and Jennifer Turnham, "Reconnecting Schools and Neighborhoods," Enterprise Community Partners Inc., 2007, www.abtassociates.com/reports/64701.pdf.

11   Karin Chenoweth, "Transforming Not Just a School But a Community," *Huffington Post*, January 6, 2014, www.huffingtonpost.com/Karin-Chenoweth/transforming-not-just-a-s_b_4549391.html.

12   Martin D. Abravanel, Robin E. Smith, and Elizabeth C. Cove, "Linking Public Housing Revitalization to Neighborhood School Improvement," Urban Institute, June 2006, www.urban.org/sites/default/files/publication/46451/411462-Linking-Public-Housing-Revitalization-to-Neighborhood-School-Improvement.PDF.

13   Brennan, "Improvements to Education."

14   Community-Wealth.org, "Overview: Anchor Institutions," http://community-wealth.org/strategies/panel/anchors/index.html.

15   Justin Glanville, "Cleveland's Greater University Circle Initiative: A Partnership between Philanthropy, Anchor Institutions and the Public Sector," Cleveland Foundation, 2013, https://www.google.com/url?sa=t&rct=j&q=&esrc=s&source=web&cd=1&cad=rja&uact=8&ved=0ahUKEwicnY_jmNDVAhXKw1QKHU-ED1MQFggqMAA&url=https%3A%2F%2Fwww.clevelandfoundation.org%2Fwp-content%2Fuploads%2F2014%2F01%2FCleveland-Foundation-Greater-University-Circle-Initiative-Case-Study-2014.pdf&usg=AFQjCNE1BgjQeiCaPMtlZn6Ckd192X9_Kg.

16   Ibid.

17   Kathryn W. Hexter, Candi Clouse, and Kenneth Kalynchuk, "Greater University Circle Initiative: Year 5 Evaluation Report," *Urban Publications*, May 2016, http://engagedscholarship.csuohio.edu/cgi/viewcontent.cgi?article=2372&context=urban_facpub.

18 Ibid.

19 Dale Maharidge, "A Photographic Chronicle of America's Working Poor," *Smithsonian*, December 2016, www.smithsonianmag.com/history/photographic-chronicle-america-working-poor-180961147/.

20 Michelle Camou, "How Urban Governments Are Promoting Worker Co-ops," Grassroots Economic Organizing, October 10, 2016, www.geo.coop/story/how-urban-governments-are-promoting-worker-co-ops.

21 Lee Chilcote, "Green City Growers Doubles Sales in the Past Year," *Crain's Cleveland Business*, August 24, 2015, www.crainscleveland.com/article/20150824/BLOGS16/150829915/green-city-growers-doubles-sales-in-the-past-year.

22 Vicki Been, "Community Benefits Agreements: A New Local Government Tool or Another Variation on the Exactions Theme?," *University of Chicago Law Review* 77, no. 1 (2010).

23 Luke Broadwater, "City Council approves $660 million bond deal for Port Covington project," *Baltimore Sun,* September 19, 2016, www.baltimoresun.com/news/maryland/baltimore-city/politics/bs-md-ci-port-covington-council-20160919-story.html.

24 Preservation Institute, "Removing Freeways—Restoring Cities: Milwaukee, Wisconsin, Park East Freeway," www.preservenet.com/freeways/FreewaysParkEast.html.

25 Ibid.

26 Laura Wolf-Powers, "Community Benefits Agreements and Local Government," *Journal of the American Planning Association* 76, no. 2, www.ci.berkeley.ca.us/uploadedFiles/Planning_and_Development/Level_3_-_Redevelopment_Agency/CBA%20and%20Local%20Government.pdf.

27 Park East Redevelopment Compact, resolution adopted by the Milwaukee County, Wisconsin, Board of Supervisors, December 16, 2014, www.forworkingfamilies.org/sites/pwf/files/documents/PERC_0.pdf.

28 Sean Ryan, "Abele: 98% of Park East Being Developed or Under Option for Sale," *Milwaukee Business Journal,* March 21, 2016, www.bizjournals.com/milwaukee/blog/real_estate/2016/03/abele-98-of-park-east-being-developed-or-under.html.

29 National Basketball Association, "Milwaukee Bucks and Alliance for Good Jobs Announce Agreement for New Arena Employees," May 19, 2016, www.nba.com/bucks/release/milwaukee-bucks-and-alliance-good-jobs-announce-agreement-new-arena-employees/.

30 Lisa Kaiser, "Leaders Applaud First-of-Its-Kind Community Benefits Agreement with Milwaukee Bucks," *Shepherd Express*, May 24, 2016, http://shepherdexpress.com/article-27871-leaders-applaud-first-of-its-kind-community-benefits-agreement-with-milwaukee-bucks-news-features.html.

31 Raj Chetty and Nathaniel Hendren, *The Impacts of Neighborhoods on Intergenerational Mobility: Childhood Exposure Effects* (Cambridge, MA: National Bureau of Economic Research, 2016); Raj Chetty, Nathaniel Hendren, Patrick Kline, and Emmanuel Saez, "Where Is the Land of Opportunity? The Geography of Intergenerational Mobility in the United States," *Quarterly Journal of Economics* 129, no. 4 (2014): 1553–1623.

32 James J. Heckman, "The Economics of Inequality: The Value of Early Childhood Education," *American Educator* 35, no. 1 (2011): 31–35.

33 Houston Independent School District, "General Information/Facts and Figures," www.houstonisd.org/domain/7908.

34 Ben Wieder, "The Most Important Award in Public Education Struggles to Find Winners," *FiveThirtyEight*, September 22, 2014, https://fivethirtyeight.com/features/the-most-important-award-in-public-education-struggles-to-find-winners/.

35 Broad Foundation, "About the Winner: Houston Independent School District," 2013, http://broadfoundation.org/wp-content/uploads/2016/03/houstonfacts.pdf.

36 Nicholas P. Morgan, "Houston Independent School District: Culture Change through Performance Pay," *District Management Journal* 4, no. 20, https://dmgroupk12.com/docmanlinks/42-dmj-04-spring-2010-1/file.

37 Ibid.

38 Kelsey Sheehy, "Houston District Named First Two-Time Broad Prize Winner," *U.S. News*, September 25, 2013, https://www.usnews.com/education/high-schools/articles/2013/09/25/houston-district-named-first-two-time-broad-prize-winner.

39 DA Custom Publishing, "Preparing Students to Enter College—and to Graduate," *DA District Administration*, October 1, 2011, https://www.districtadministration.com/article/preparing-students-enter-college-%E2%80%94-and-graduate.

40 Sheehy, "Houston District Named."

41 DA Custom Publishing, "Preparing Students."

42 Christina A. Samuels, "Houston Schools Take a Page from Best Charters," *Education Week*, March 5, 2012, www.edweek.org/ew/articles/2012/03/07/23biz-charter.h31.html?r=279464225.

43 Richard Carranza, "2017 State of the Schools," speech at Hilton Americas-Houston Hotel, Houston, February 15, 2017, www.houstonisd.org/site/default.aspx?PageType=3&ModuleInstanceID=230668&ViewID=7B97F7ED-8E5E-4120-848F-A8B4987D588F&RenderLoc=0&FlexDataID=194203&PageID=158769.

44 Raj Chetty, Nathaniel Hendren, and Lawrence F. Katz, "The Effects of Exposure to Better Neighborhoods on Children: New Evidence from the Moving to Opportunity Experiment," *American Economic Review*, 106, no. 4 (2016): 855–902.

45 Susan J. Popkin, Laura E. Harris, and Mary K. Cunningham, "Families in Transition: A Qualitative Analysis of the MTO Experience: Final Report," U.S. Department of Housing and Urban Development, Office of Policy Development and Research, 2002, https://www.huduser.gov/Publications/pdf/mtoqualf.pdf.

46 Montgomery County, Maryland, Department of Housing and Community Affairs, executive regulation 13-05AM, "Moderately Priced Dwelling Unit Program," effective September 28, 2005, www.montgomerycountymd.gov/DHCA/Resources/Files/housing/singlefamily/mpdu/execreg_13-05am.pdf.

47 Fairfax County, Virginia, government, "Tysons Comprehensive Plan Amendments, 2013–2015," www.fairfaxcounty.gov/tysons/comprehensiveplan.

48 Heather L. Schwartz, Liisa Ecola, Kristin Leuschner, and Aaron Kofner, *Is Inclusionary Zoning Inclusionary? A Guide for Practitioners* (Santa Monica, CA: Rand Corporation, 2012), www.rand.org/pubs/technical_reports/TR1231.html.

49 Diane K. Levy, Kaitlin Franks, Kassie Bertumen, and Martin Abravanel, *Expanding Housing Opportunities through Inclusionary Zoning: Lessons from Two Counties*, U.S. Department of Housing and Urban Development, Office of Policy Development and Research, December 2012, https://www.huduser.gov/portal/publications/HUD-496_new.pdf.

50 Fairfax County, Virginia, Office of Community Revitalization, *Tysons 2015–2016 Progress Report on the Implementation of the Comprehensive Plan*, October 2016, www.fairfaxcounty.gov/tysons/implementation/download/2016_annualreport_final.pdf.

51 Robert Hickey, "Inclusionary Upzoning: Tying Growth to Affordability," Inclusionary Housing series, National Housing Conference's Center for Housing Policy, July 2014, http://media.wix.com/ugd/19cfbe_4c2a9adc5ccd4ca181f8b434b2a5b8f6.pdf.

52 Christopher B. Leinberger, "DC: The Walk Up Wake-Up Call," George Washington University School of Business, 2012, https://www.smartgrowthamerica.org/app/legacy/documents/Walkup-report.pdf.

53 Katherine Shaver, "Suburbs seeking transit look for ways to keep residents from being priced out," *Washington Post*, November 28, 2016, https://www.washingtonpost.com/local/trafficandcommuting/suburbs-seeking-transit-look-for-ways-to-keep-residents-from-being-priced-out/2016/11/28/110d5b6c-b01d-11e6-840f-e3ebab6bcdd3_story.html?utm_term=.7fa47de082be.

54 For more information on housing trust funds, see the Housing Trust Fund Project of the Center for Community Change, https://housingtrustfundproject.org/.

55 Lance Freeman, "Displacement or Succession? Residential Mobility in Gentrifying Neighborhoods," *Urban Affairs Review* 40, no. 4 (2005).

56 Jeffrey Lubell, "Preserving and Expanding Affordability in Neighborhoods Experiencing Rising Rents and Property Values," *Cityscape* 18, no. 3 (2016).

57 Allison Allbee, Rebecca Johnson, and Jeffrey Lubell, *Preserving, Protecting & Expanding Affordable Housing: A Policy Toolkit for Public Health* (Oakland, CA: ChangeLab Solutions, 2015).

58 Urban Land Conservancy, "Denver Transit-Oriented Development Fund," www.urbanlandc.org/denver-transit-oriented-development-fund.

59 Richard Metcalf, "Sawmill District Enjoying Renaissance," *Albuquerque Journal*, February 17, 2014, https://www.abqjournal.com/354227/sawmill-district-enjoying-renaissance.html.

60 Associated Press, "Alamogordo Sawmill Closes, Leaving 70 Unemployed," *Albuquerque Journal*, October 20, 2007, https://www.abqjournal.com/news/state/apsawmill10-20-07.htm.

61 Teresa Russin, "The Community Land Trust Model and Smart Growth Principles as a Means to Provide Affordable Housing in the Face of Gentrification," (master's thesis, University of Florida, 2007), http://etd.fcla.edu/UF/UFE0021792/russin_t.pdf.

62 Miriam Axel-Lute and Dana Hawkins-Simons, "Community Land Trusts Grown from Grassroots," Lincoln Institute of Land Policy, July 2015, https://www.lincolninst.edu/es/publications/articles/community-land-trusts-grown-grassroots.

63 Kenneth Temkin, Brett Theodos, and David Price, *Balancing Affordability and Opportunity: An Evaluation of Affordable Homeownership Programs with Long-term Affordability Controls* (Washington, DC: Urban Institute, 2010).

64 See "Harris County PY 2016 Request for Proposals Application Guidebook for HOME Investment Partnerships Program (HOME)," www.harriscountytx.gov/CmpDocuments/103/RFP/PY2016_HC_AFF_HOUS_HOME_RFP_Guidebook_FINAL_040516.pdf.

65 Tom White, Charlie Wilkins, and Edward J. Pinto, "Economical Rental Housing by Design for Communities That Work" (Washington, DC: American Enterprise Institute International Center on Housing Risk, 2016).

66 Elijah Chiland, "New state rules make it easier to build in-law units in Los Angeles," *Curbed Los Angeles*, January 9, 2017, https://la.curbed.com/2017/1/9/14219298/granny-flats-new-rules-state-back-house-in-law.

67 Martha M. Galvez, *What Do We Know about Housing Choice Voucher Program Location Outcomes? A Review of Recent Literature* (Washington, DC: What Works Collaborative, 2010); Deborah J. Devine, Robert W. Gray, Lester Rubin, and Lydia B. Taghavi, *Housing Choice Voucher Location Patterns: Implications for Participants and Neighborhood Welfare* (Washington, DC: U.S. Department of Housing and Urban Development, 2003).

68 Housing Opportunity Through Modernization Act of 2016 (HOTMA).

69 King County Washington Housing Authority, "Key Facts," https://www.kcha.org/about/facts.

70 King County Office of Performance Strategy and Budget, "King County Comprehensive Plan," Attachment A to Ordinance 18427," December 5, 2016, www.kingcounty.gov/-/media/depts/executive/performance-strategy-budget/regional-planning/2016CompPlanUpdate/2016Adopted-KCCP/KingCountyCompPlan-ADO-120516.ashx?la=en.

71 King County Office of Performance Strategy and Budget, "2016 King County Comprehensive Plan Update," Technical Appendix B: Housing, September 1, 2016, www.kingcounty.gov/-/media/Council/documents/CompPlan/2016/striker/Attachment-D-to-S1-Appendix-B-Housing-2016-KCCP-090116.ashx?la=en.

72 King County Housing Authority, "Moving to Work: FY 2017 Annual Plan," 2016, https://portal.hud.gov/hudportal/documents/huddoc?id=kingcounty17plan.pdf.

73 Enterprise Community Partners, "Regional Equitable Development Initiative (REDI) Fund," www.enterprisecommunity.org/financing-and-development/community-loan-fund/redi-fund.

CHAPTER 4

1   Bridgespan Group, "Needle-Moving Community Collaboratives Case Study: Cincinnati, Covington, and Newport," https://www.bridgespan.org/bridgespan/Images/articles/needle-moving-community-collaboratives/profiles/community-collaboratives-case-study-cinncinnati.pdf.

2   David Bornstein, "Coming Together to Give Schools a Boost," *New York Times,* March 7, 2011, https://opinionator.blogs.nytimes.com/2011/03/07/coming-together-to-give-schools-a-boost/.

3   Rockefeller Foundation, "Strive Together: Taking a place-based network to national scale," http://engage.rockefellerfoundation.org/story-sketch/strive/.

4   Diane Elliott, "Financially Insecure Residents Can Cost Cities Millions," Urban Institute's *Urban Wire: Neighborhoods, Cities, and Metros*, January 24, 2017, www.urban.org/urban-wire/financially-insecure-residents-can-cost-cities-millions.

5   StriveTogether, "The Network," www.strivetogether.org/cradle-career-network.

6   Alan Berube and Benjamin Forman, "A Local Ladder for the Working Poor: The Impact of the Earned Income Tax Credit in U.S. Metropolitan Areas," Brookings Institution, September 2001, https://www.brookings.edu/wp-content/uploads/2016/06/eitcnational.pdf.

7   For more information, see Center for Financial Inclusion, "Enabling Financial Capability Along the Road to Financial Inclusion," www.centerforfinancialinclusion.org/fi2020/roadmap-to-inclusion/financial-capability.

8   Consumer Financial Protection Board, "Financial Well-Being: The Goal of Financial Education," January 2015, http://files.consumerfinance.gov/f/201501_cfpb_report_financial-well-being.pdf.

9   Diana Elliott, Caroline Ratcliffe, and Emma Cancian Kalish, "The Financial Health of Detroit Residents," Urban Institute, October 12, 2016, www.urban.org/research/publication/financial-health-detroit-residents.

10 Reid Cramer, Rourke O'Brien, Daniel Cooper, and Maria Luengo-Prado, "A Penny Saved Is Mobility Earned: Advancing Economic Mobility through Savings" (Washington, DC: Economic Mobility Project, an initiative of the Pew Charitable Trusts, 2009), www.pewtrusts.org/-/media/legacy/uploadedfiles/pcs_assets/2009/empsavingsreportpdf.pdf.

11 Marsha Mercer, "Children's Savings Accounts Help States Create 'College-Going Culture,'" *Stateline*, Pew Charitable Trusts, April 6, 2015, www.pewtrusts.org/en/research-and-analysis/blogs/stateline/2015/4/06/childrens-savings-account-help-states-create-college-going-culture.

12 Mayor Michael R. Bloomberg, 2006 State of the City address, "A Blueprint for New York City's Future," January 26, 2006, http://www1.nyc.gov/office-of-the-mayor/news/030-06/mayor-michael-bloomberg-delivers-2006-state-the-city-address-a-blueprint-new-york-city-s.

13 Diane Cardwell, "New Office Would Battle City Poverty," *New York Times,* December 19, 2006, http://query.nytimes.com/gst/fullpage.html?res=9E06EED91331F93AA-25751C1A9609C8B63.

14 City of New York Department of Consumer Affairs, Programs, https://www1.nyc.gov/site/dca/partners/programs.page.

15 City Hall Press Office, "City's Expanded Tax Credit Campaign Pays off Big for New Yorkers," City of New York, April 15, 2015, http://www1.nyc.gov/office-of-the-mayor/news/242-15/city-s-expanded-tax-credit-campaign-pays-off-big-new-yorkers.

16 NYC Department of Consumer Affairs, "NYC Department of Consumer Affairs Office of Financial Empowerment: Progress Report, 2010–2013," New York City government, December 2013, https://www1.nyc.gov/assets/dca/downloads/pdf/partners/Research-OFEProgressReport20102013.pdf.

17 Bloomberg Philanthropies, "Bloomberg Philanthropies and Living Cities' CFE Fund Announce Five Cities Selected for $16.2 M In Financial Empowerment Center Grants," January 8, 2013, https://www.bloomberg.org/press/releases/bloomberg-philanthropies-and-living-cities-cfe-fund-announce-five-cities-selected-for-16-2-m-in-financial-empowerment-center-grants/.

18 Cities for Financial Empowerment Fund, "Our Impact," http://cfefund.org.

19 Kahliah Laney, David Giles, and Jonathan Bowles, "Innovations to Build On," Center for an Urban Future, November 2013, https://nycfuture.org/pdf/Innovations-to-Build-On.pdf.

20 Jonathan Mintz, "How Financial Empowerment Can Save Cities Money: The Supervitamin Effect,'" *Governing,* September 5, 2013*,* www.governing.com/blogs/view/col-cities-financial-counseling-empowerment-supervitamin-effect.html.

21 JP Morgan Chase & Co., "New Skills at Work: Growing Skills for a Growing Chicago—Strengthening the Middle-Skill Workforce in the City That Works," 2015, https://www.jpmorganchase.com/corporate/Corporate-Responsibility/chicago-skills-gap-report.htm.

22 For a summary of lessons learned from earlier workforce efforts and the career pathways approach, see appendices 7.1 and 7.2 in U.S. Department of Housing and Urban Development, *Administering an Effective Family Self-Sufficiency Program: A Guidebook Based on Evidence and Promising Practices* (Washington, DC: HUD, 2017). See also Alan Werner, Catherine Dun Rappaport, Jennifer Bagnell Stuart, and Jennifer Lewis, "Literature Review: Career Pathways Programs (OPRE Report #2013-24)," prepared by Abt Associates for U.S. Department of Health and Human Services' Administration for Children and Families, Office of Planning, Research, and Evaluation, June 24, 2013, https://www.acf.hhs.gov/sites/default/files/opre/cp_lit_review_final_62613_edits.pdf.

23 Deborah Kobes and Ian Rosenblum, "Growing Skills for a Growing Chicago: Strengthening the Middle-Skill Workforce in the City that Works," JPMorgan Chase & Co., June 2015, https://www.jpmorganchase.com/corporate/Corporate-Responsibility/document/54841-jpmc-gap-chicago-aw3-v2-accessible.pdf.

24 Alexia Elejalde-Ruiz, "Learning middle-skills to snag living wages," *Chicago Tribune,* June 8, 2015*,* www.chicagotribune.com/business/ct-jp-morgan-chase-middle-skill-jobs-0609-biz-20150608-story.html.

25 Matt Helmer and Amy Blair, "Courses to Employment: Sectoral Approaches to Community College–Nonprofit Partnerships," Aspen Institute, February 2011, www.aspenwsi.org/wordpress/wp-content/uploads/11-002.pdf.

26 Elizabeth Copson, Karin Martinson, and Karen Gardiner, "Pace Career Pathways Program Profile: Instituto del Progreso Latino, Carreras en Salud," U.S. Department of Health and Human Services Office of Planning, Research, and Evaluation, March 2014, http://abtassociates.com/AbtAssociates/files/b2/b2dd02fa-9ebf-4804-88e1-33784cad7f3f.pdf.

27 Raisa Bruner, "The American Dream Isn't Dead. This is How Immigrant Families are Achieving It," NationSwell, November 9, 2015, http://nationswell.com/juan-salgado-instituto-latino-american-dream-success.

28 Career Pathways, "Overview: What Is a Career Pathway?" www.career-pathways.org/about-career-pathways.

29 Frank A. Mirabal, "Carreras en Salud: A Chicago Bilingual Health Care Career Pathways Partnership," National Council of La Raza, 2008, http://ww1.insightcced.org/uploads/assets/Lopez,%20Simon/CarrerasEnSalud.pdf.

30 Oscar Perry Abello, "Chicago Job Training Program Changes Minds (and the Rules)," *Next City,* October 7, 2015, https://nextcity.org/daily/entry/chicago-job-training-manufacturing-placement-juan-salgado-macarthur.

31 Lili Gil Valletta, "Latina Entrepreneurs Elevate Minority Business Issues during Meeting with President Trump," *Huffington Post*, March 27, 2017, www.huffingtonpost.com/entry/latina-entrepreneurs-elevate-issues-and-opportunities_us_58d9744be4b0e6062d922ff0.

32 JPMorgan Chase & Co. and the Initiative for a Competitive Inner City, "The Big Impact of Small Businesses on Urban Job Creation: Evidence from Five Cities," October 2016, http://icic.org/wp-content/uploads/2016/10/JPMC_R1_BigImpact_FINAL_forpost.pdf.

33 See, for example, Sarah Treuhaft and Victor Rubin, "Economic Inclusion: Advancing an Equity-Driven Growth Model," Big Ideas for Job Creation Project, https://www.noexperiencenecessarybook.com/25p71/economic-inclusion-advancing-an-equity-driven-policylink.html.

34 JPMorgan Chase & Co. and ICIC, "Accelerating Cluster Growth: A Playbook for City Leaders," June 2015, http://icic.org/wp-content/uploads/2016/04/ICIC_JPMC_AcceleratingClusterGrowth_ExecutiveSummary_final_v2.pdf.

35 Iris Dimmick, "Microlender Accion Texas Rebrands to LiftFund," LiftFund, January 14, 2015, www.liftfund.com/news/microlender-accion-texas-rebrands-liftfund.

36 "FAQ," LiftFund San Antonio, http://sanantonio.liftfund.com/faq.

37 Chris Peak, "This Unconventional Lender Fulfills the Entrepreneurial Dreams of Those with Poor Credit," NationSwell, March 2, 2016, http://nationswell.com/liftfund-micro-lender-poor-credit-business-owners/#ixzz4XSxZpPQq.

38 Jacob Wascalus, "CDFIs seek to innovate to compete with speedy online lenders," Federal Reserve Bank of Minneapolis, November 10, 2015, https://www.minneapolisfed.org/publications/community-dividend/cdfis-seek-to-innovate-to-compete-with-speedy-online-lenders.

39 JPMorgan Chase & Co. and LiftFund, "JPMorgan Chase & Co. and LiftFund Announce New Program to Increase Access to Capital for Minority and Women-owned Small Businesses," news release, October 11, 2016, www.liftfund.com/wp-content/uploads/2016/10/NR-LiftFund-Chase-Dallas.pdf.

40 San Antonio Hispanic Chamber of Commerce, "LiftFund and the City of San Antonio Celebrate Cafe Commerce's Stellar First Year," September 17, 2015, www.sahcc.org/membership/liftfund-and-the-city-of-san-antonio-celebrate-cafe-commerces-stellar-first-year.

41 Tony Quesada, "San Antonio Chamber, Café Commerce partner on small-business coaching program," *San Antonio Business Journal,* September 2, 2015, www.bizjournals.com/sanantonio/news/2015/09/02/san-antonio-chamber-caf-commerce-partner-on-small.html.

42 Steven R. Nivin, "Economic and Fiscal Impacts of LiftFund: 2010–2015," April 2016, www.liftfund.com/wp-content/uploads/2016/05/LiftFund-Economic-Impact-Study-2010-2015.pdf.

CHAPTER 5

1   Ron Nirenberg, "For Equity's Sake, a Fair Budget," *San Antonio Express-News*, August 22, 2017.

2   Envision Utah, "Preparing for Community Engagement," www.envisionutah.org/community-engagement/item/167.

3   Max Blau, "Reed: To make Atlanta great, we must focus on equity," *Atlanta*, February 11, 2016, www.atlantamagazine.com/news-culture-articles/267792/.

4   Interview with the authors.

5   Blau, "Reed."

6   Kasim Reed, State of the City address, Georgia World Congress Center, Atlanta, February 4, 2016, https://www.youtube.com/watch?v=Qbs16PD83j4.

7   Interview with the authors.

8   National League of Cities, "NLC President Matt Zone Creates Economic Mobility and Opportunity Task Force," National League of Cities, news release, November 21, 2016, www.nlc.org/article/nlc-president-matt-zone-creates-economic-mobility-and-opportunity-task-force.

9   Interview with the authors.

10   Interview with the authors.

11   Jennifer Dixon, "How Detroit is helping inmates prepare for jobs," *Detroit Free Press*, January 22, 2017, www.freep.com/story/news/local/michigan/detroit/2017/01/22/behind-bars-training-help-detroit-inmates-find-jobs-construction/96349828/.

12   Christine Ferretti, "Jobs, neighborhoods, housing take focus in Duggan's speech," *Detroit News*, February 21, 2017, www.detroitnews.com/story/news/local/detroit-city/2017/02/21/neighborhoods-still-focus-duggan-readies-speech/98178388/.

APPENDIX

1   Some would argue that earnings should be tracked instead of income because income includes elements like interest on savings that are not a primary focus of economic mobility efforts. Data on income, however, are generally easier to obtain than data on earnings and are a reasonable substitute. The illustrative measures here, therefore, focus on income.

2   The average income of households in the bottom half of the income distribution is more useful than the average income for the entire population for tracking gains from policies and programs because the overall average can be affected heavily by gains among the highest earners. Tracking the *median* income for the entire population is more useful than tracking the *average* income for the entire population, but may not be indicative of what is happening among households in the bottom half of the income distribution.

3   It is also important to ensure that the minimum standards being used for measurement are not defined in a way that holds the share of students passing them to a constant share of the overall student population.

4   The U.S Department of Housing and Urban Development defines a very low-income household as one with income at or below 50 percent of the area median income.

5   Given the sizable effects that high-quality schools and teachers have on individuals' life opportunities (see Raj Chetty and Nathaniel Hendren, *The Impacts of Neighborhoods on Intergenerational Mobility: Childhood Exposure Effects* [Cambridge, MA: National Bureau of Economic Research, 2016], and Raj Chetty, Nathaniel Hendren, Patrick Kline, and Emmanuel Saez, "Where Is the Land of Opportunity? The Geography of Intergenerational Mobility in the United States," *Quarterly Journal of Economics* 129, no. 4 [2014]: 1553–1623), it is important to measure the affordability of housing in neighborhoods with good schools as well as to measure educational achievement directly. Improvement in educational achievement among low-income households can occur for a numbers of reasons, including improvement in the quality of schools located in low-income neighborhoods, as well as improved access by low-income households to neighborhoods with high-quality schools. Unless the ability of low-income households to live in areas with good schools is measured separately, it will be difficult to know if improved educational achievement is attributable to one or the other of these factors. Ideally, an equitable city would experience gains through both mechanisms.

6   A number of opportunity indices are available. For example, diversitydatakids.org has developed a Child Opportunity Index for the 100 largest metropolitan areas. Diversitydatakids.org is a partnership of the Institute for Child, Youth, and Family Policy at the Heller School at Brandeis University and the Kirwan Institute for the Study of Race and Ethnicity at Ohio State University. Enterprise Community Partners has also developed an opportunity index that was expected to be made available in 2017 for communities around the United States. In order to measure progress in expanding the availability of affordable housing in opportunity areas, it is important that cities use opportunity measures that do not themselves include housing affordability.

7   The tool is available at https://egis.hud.gov/affht.